//
[bon aire projects]

ISBN-13: 978-0-9915820-0-6

This project is supported in part by the generous funding of the Gray Chair
(Steve McCaffery), the McNulty Chair (Dennis Tedlock), and the English Depart-
ment at SUNY Buffalo.

www.bonaireprojects.com

HOLLY MELGARD'S FRIENDS & FAMILY

Joey Yearous-Algozin

INTRODUCTION
Teresa Carmody / Vanessa Place

//

[bon aire projects]

/ INTRODUCTION BY TERESA CARMODY[1] /

---

1   Footnotes by Vanessa Place

"In these days, when we have decided, as it seems, that nothing is to be forgotten, two things are rapidly becoming essential—some literary condensing machine, and a system of indexing."
        —Leslie Stephen, "Biography," The National Review 22.128, 1893

I don't know Holly Melgard, though I know of a young poet named Holly Melgard who lives in New York and is part of the Troll Thread Collective.[2] I also know she is either enrolled in or has completed the Poetics program at SUNY Buffalo, and that she dates[3] Joey Yearous-Algozin.[4] These facts, though limited, are enough to establish the reality of a person named Holly Melgard, a person who likely would (based on what I know of the young conceptualists in New York and their interest, as hearsay has it, in confessional-conceptual practices) allow her boyfriend access to her voicemail for three years, so to transcribe the messages—perhaps all of them, perhaps selections—to create this present volume: *Holly Melgard's Friends & Family* by Joey Yearous-Algozin.[5]

The fact of Holly Melgard's existence provides the absent presence at the center of the book. It grounds the messages as true

---

2   Kristen Gallagher asked Holly Melgard why she performed childbirth in a 2013 essay for Jacket2; Melgard discussed the construction of labor as a site-non-site of the construction of the subject, and ultimately responded, "Why not childbirth?" https://jacket2.org/commentary/why-childbirth

3   The author is referring to "dating," generally understood as to go out with someone socially, or to spend time with romantically. It may be that this reference also works to temporally mark or situate Holly Melgard at the time of this writing, as a relative dating method (such as seriation or dendrochronology) or as a kind of written marker (such as epigraphy or palaeography).

4   See e.g., https://jacket2.org/category/commentary-tags/joey-yearous-algozin

5   This project has its most obvious predecessor in Gertrude Stein's *The Autobiography of Alice B. Toklas.* Of course, Stein's circle was extraordinarily cosmopolitan, a collection of genius, both literary and artistic, the leading lights of their generation, and frankly, of generations yet to come. It is interesting to note that autobiography, which this may or may not be, was originally considered to be a form of apologia, or self-justification rather than self-documentation. By using Melgard's voicemail messages, or addresses from specific others rather than the generalized address of the biography or autobiography, it appears that *HMFF* is conflating these two modes of the form.

and gives the messengers a reason to speak: they want to com-municate with Holly Melgard, their real-life daughter, sister, edi-tor, teacher, girlfriend, friend, etc.[6] And her existence makes their speech as true as their *ums* and *uhs*, even as these verbalized pauses and non-lexical sounds contribute to the text's documentary-style realness.[7] Likewise, the lack of punctuation authenticates the text's verbal origins; we don't, after all, say *comma comma em dash* when we speak. If Holly Melgard were an immediate fiction, the reader would wonder, from the beginning and more pointedly, about her absence. For as a fiction, this absence would be a formal choice filled with generic implications and metaphoric significance. But as a true, live person, Holly Melgard's voicemail becomes a contem-porary window we can peek into with a voyeur's[8] delight and lack of narrative expectation.

And what do we see but her family and friends.[9] We see their patterns—when they call and what they say. Their jokes, worries, and verbal tics. Their health problems and pathologies. The kinds

---

6   See fn. 4, ante. Though this is a tautological argument, given that mes-sages are on the one hand always "true" insofar as they reveal the desire of the author to be seen as the origin of that message, and on the other hand, may or may not be "true" in any ontological factual fashion. Thus, they participate in a kind of "facticity" which can be usefully distinguished from fact.

7   "Realness" may refer to either a sense of objective reality or to a per-formance of authenticity, such as in the drag community. Realness in the latter sense has come to mean an interior projection of appropriated per-formativity into an exterior field of play.

8   The voyeur, according to Jacques-Alain Miller, imports the gaze to "ob-struct the hole in the Other," and thereby make the Other whole. The voyeur creates the Other as an instrument of his jouissance. See Josefina Ayerza. "Jacques-Alain Miller's Perversion," *Lacanian Ink*. http://www.lacan.com/frame11.htm The question here is whether it is Yearous-Algozin or the reader who is the primary voyeur: it could be argued that, as Yearous-Algozin was given individual permission to listen to and transcribe these documents, he is in the position of another Other for our regard. On the other hand, so to speak, it could be that we are being voyeur-ed by both the author and the purported subject—caught watching, caught spying, in the Sartrean sense. In which case we would be using the text object here to create our own corporeal subjectivity via our sense of shame at our own otherness—our own sense of being yet another body for others in a series of cohesive (affective) political social networks.

9   Idem.

of things they want to talk about (as opposed to sending an email), and the ways they socialize with and relate to Holly Melgard, who becomes, as the book continues, increasingly fictional. For these are not Holly Melgard's voicemail messages, but representations thereof, and as such, they are an artifice whose truth lies in the imaginary.

I don't know Holly Melgard. Nor do I know her friends and family. But here, in this book, is an excellent cast of characters to engage your sympathies and test your loyalties. You will, undoubtedly, come to know some characters better than others; you may worry about certain ones and psychologize others. You may, like I did, pick a favorite. And a favorite joke.[10]

---

10 Such as: What's the difference between a brothel and your mum's house?
Your mum's house is a lovely place; a safe haven where I can take a much needed break from the troubles of the world. She waits on me hand and foot, really pulling out all the stops to make me feel welcome. Between her and your dad, it's a home away from home.
A brothel is where I fuck your sister.

/ HOLLY MELGARD'S FRIENDS & FAMILY /

Ellie // 1/1/11

hey Hollster um just giving you a call happy New Year happy twenty eleven um we by the way um the card is amazing probably my favorite part of the present um and the sake set is very beautiful I'm going to use it tomorrow um and drink the shit out of that sake just so in case you were wondering but I miss you I really hope you had a good New Year's and we should set up a friend date or something because we need to talk so um I'll talk to you soon bye

Parents // 1/2/11

hi Holly this is Mom guess what the refrigerator died well let me put it this way it smelled like something was burning and so I called the fire department and they they said that there was um it was too hot around the outside of it the the seams up on on top and in other places so it sounds it sounds like you know they didn't say this but it sounds like a fan some motor is burning out anyway um possibly the fan whatever the fan the fan goes out then the whole thing can get way too hot but anyways so anyway we had to turn it unplug it and um tomorrow we're gonna have to go pursue a search for a refrigerator of all things that's the last that's I mean ha anyways aye aye aye talk to you later love you sweetie not your problem it's ours we'll deal with it it'll come out fine one way or the other take care

Divya // 1/3/11

hey Holls it's me um I think you referred to me as Miss Bergamo uh I'm not sure but I guess that's me I called you earlier with two intents one to see if you wanted to hang out which is awesome that you wanted to do the same so let's get together tonight secondly we were on campus and there was a package for you and I wanted to know if you wanted me to pick it up but it is too late so I'm now back home uh anyways call me back and let's make plans ciao

Parents // 1/4/11

Holly this is your mom I am just shaking I am so upset I got a call from um it was this um insurance company um and the woman from the [identifying information redacted] or something and she said that on December twenty-third our car struck another vehicle and this was in a parking lot and that the the other people they took down the license plate number they followed the car and there was nobody in the car at the time and um and they took the license plate number and the description of the car and so they filed the report with the police and they said that it was a female driver and the question is what were you doing at that time were you with Dad in downtown uh downtown or or what was happening this is twenty-third of December and um I and and so the question is so I said well there is nobody here that could have done that but then I don't know I don't know what you are the only other female that would have driven our car I have no idea but I need to I need you to call me at work I'm going to be at work today and I I am so upset that I am just shaking I mean they could sue us they I mean we don't have a lot of money Holly we don't need this I mean if you have to drop out of graduate school to pay for this yourself I mean I I don't want to threaten you but I am just I am just sick I mean what the hell is this and maybe it wasn't you and maybe it I shouldn't blame you and um I'm going to try to call Michael at work too but I just want to get to the root of this and find out what the hell is happening here

Ellie // 1/5/11
oh hey I accidentally hung up on you call me back bye

Parents // 1/5/11
hi Holly um the insurance adjuster did not call today ok so I just wanted to let you know that ok so um and and I'm sorry we weren't home but I had to get the money out of the bank to go and get the refrigerator so I paid for the refrigerator and it will be coming next Tuesday in the morning and ok

Joey // 1/7/11
hey babe it's me um I'm over at Chris' with Chris and Matt um just seeing what you're doing seeing if you wanted to hang out so I love you give me a call soon ok bye

Parents // 1/9/11
um oh just anyways an update take care talk to you later bye

Nick // 1/11/11
hey what's up Holly it's Nick um just trying you back again I tried you last night um and didn't get you I'll be in class for a good part of the rest of the day but um in and out so uh give me a call alright bye

Parents // 1/14/11

hi Holly um let's see uh yeah give me a call everything's cool um that adjuster woman called back and she said that she looked at the photos and the photos were clear enough she said she did see some little you know little tiny dent but it was clear that that was there before and uh you know whatever so um in any case um uh yeah so I guess that's it if you have any other questions give me a call and um now all we can do is just wait and you know it's not the end of the world anyway life goes on and and we just you know anyway it just anyway ok I love you take care

Parents // 1/30/11

Holly this is Mom I'm trying to get the um my the food processor you gave me to just make slices and so far I've got it shredded I've got it diced I've got it everything else and I can't get it to do just that so I'm going to end up doing them all by hand because I just can't figure it out I can't find the booklet that tells how to do it anyway talk to you later bye

Chris // 2/5/11

hey dude it's me uh I just wanted to call and say thanks for having me over last night and thanks again for feeding me uh it was an awesome time and I'm so glad that we got together and talked for like eight hours um just really necessary though god eight hours um we should have recorded it as you mentioned um yeah I was just calling also to see if you guys got Tobin's email about possibly coming over and watching the Super Bowl tomorrow evening um we would love to have you I know Joey uh just has to watch the Packers I guess I guess it's in his blood or so he says um and also I hope he's ok I know he more than likely is but I just wanted to check with you and see that he was doing alright we were yelling at each other last night which never really happens and so um you know I fully integrated the thing into my consciousness and in no way am feeling like something was broken last night in any terms but you know I just want to make sure that Joey knows that it was all the spirit of the discourse and I wasn't really angry at him so I hope he's not really angry at me ok uh I love you guys and call me whenever you get this bye

Marg // 2/12/11

hey Holly it's Margaret um I wanted to know if you and Joey wanted to meet up with all of us for um brunch at Betty's that would be probably Joel and Thom and me uh anyway we're going to head there in about ten minutes so um see you soon hopefully ok bye

Parents // 3/6/11

Holly guess what I'm really using lee leaks l-e-a-k-s lately they are so delicious they're maybe it's l-e-e-k-s I think it's l-e-e-k-s oh my god they are so delicious I have to tell you how um I don't think so I'm talking to the answering machine Ed anyway but I wanted to tell you about that and I'm upping the garlic I'm using my new garlic press and oh boy I made this spaghetti tonight pretty good I'll tell you and I used fresh um um Italian parsley flat leaf parsley oh my god chopped up lots of it um delicious mushrooms leeks garlic and Italian parsley oh my god so good as a topping for spaghetti oh my god talk to you later bye bye

David // 3/17/11

hey Holly this is David uh a couple of things uh I wanted to make sure you knew that John is driving next week so as I said we'd be leaving at ten so I need to get your address at some point so we know where to get you that morning uh as for the question I asked you about asking Steve or Dennis for some cash yeah don't worry about that I'm really I shouldn't have asked you to do that I just felt that uh Steve has already funded so many various things that I'm involved in that I don't feel that asking him but I shouldn't have uh shoved that on on to you so we'll figure something out um anyway I look forward to going to get on the road and talk to you about it soon give me a call if you've got any questions hope you're well bye

Joey // 3/23/11

hey I'm in my office uh come to my office ok bye

Parents // 3/31/11

hi Holly it's Mom um oh I have to work today I'll give you a call later I get off at ten so it's going to be awfully late your time um one way or the other we'll be in touch love you sweetie how's the three legged kitty anyway or Crayon how's Crayon how are you love you sweetie pie hugs and kisses and lots of cookies bye bye chocolate chip with walnuts bye bye

Jeremiah // 4/1/11

hey Holly it's me um I uh just got done teaching and I was uh calling to check in see if you needed a ride or anything um because I'm about to head over to the uh Bernadette Mayer thing otherwise um but yeah if you're stuck at the shop or whatever let me know and I'll uh I'll come grab you and bring you back here if you want or wherever um ok hope you're well bye

Rae // 4/1/11

hey Holly it's me sorry I missed all your calls I've been running around like a maniac all morning and left my cell phone at home I hope your ok um please call me when you get a chance I'm going to worry about you a little bit ok um I really hope you're alright ok bye

Mechanic // 4/1/11

Good afternoon Holly it's Dennis from the collision shop your car is all set if you want to give me a call it's [identifying information redacted] that's [identifying information redacted] area code [identifying information redacted] thank you

Frannie // 4/1/11

hey Holly um this is Frannie Banny calling um I know you're busy right now and I know you've got a lot of stuff going on and I'm not in any crisis or anything like that but I could just use someone to talk to if you just have a few minutes so um so if you get a minute um I would be very ecstatic to have a few minutes to uh just bounce some things off of you so um yeah whenever you get the chance um or whenever is more convenient for you um it would mean a lot for me to hear from you ok thanks love you lots and I'll talk to you soon hopefully ok sweetheart thanks bye

Aaron // 4/2/11

hi Holly it's Aaron and uh I'm trying to get uh in touch with Conrad um uh about uh some plans for tomorrow uh so uh if uh for some reason I lost Joey's number but I left a message for Robbie um too uh but um if you could help me out it would be appreciated thanks bye

Joey // 4/5/11
hey it's me um give me a call when you get a chance ok bye

Parents // 4/13/11
Holly I have a song to play for you

Sarah // 4/19/11
hey Holly um this is Sarah sorry we got cut off um my phone just died I just ran home to plug it in um uh but it's plugged in now so when you get this feel free to call me back or else I'll try again in a couple minutes um my number is [identifying information redacted] ok talk to you soon bye

Brother // 4/21/11
what's up little nigga it's your brother I'm just seeing what you're doing so I don't know it's not real important or nothing so if you're real busy call me tomorrow or whenever so talk to you later bye

Katie // 4/29/11
Holly this is Katie I need to speak to you immediately I have something to tell you that's very very important and uh need some immediate attention and some top secret advice so um if you could call me back whenever that would be awesome ok bye

Katie // 4/29/11
ok I'm sorry I just wanted to call you twice because I wanted you to know that I've never called you twice and never asked for immediate call back um so this is important alright bye

Parents // 5/8/11
hi Holly it's Mom just give me a call when you get a chance wait an hour so ok it's now almost three bye love you sweetie

AJ // 5/10/11
hello Hollister it's AJ um I'm just calling long time no talk uh sorry um everything's been hectic and horrible over here and I'm sure

you've been very busy as well anyways I'm thinking about you miss you and love you and um just want to catch up next time we both have a chance I'm driving to Olympia right now actually so I'll be in my car for an hour so when you get this call me back alright love you bye

Frannie // 5/17/11
Holly Melgard this is Fran [identifying information redacted] if this is your number which I hope to god that it is um I'm really missing out on some Holly-isms so if you could call me back I would greatly appreciate it I would love to hear from you so my phone number is [identifying information redacted] call me love ya bye

Parents // 5/18/11
yeah Holly it's your dad your brother wants you to call him he didn't pay his phone bill and he wants to say hi it's Friday at ten to one

Parents // 5/18/11
hi Holly Michael wants you to call him ok love you sweetie bye bye

[identifying information redacted] // 5/20/11
hi this message is for Holly this is the doctor's office calling you could pick up your prescription after one o'clock today the office will be open till six thank you

[identifying information redacted] // 5/20/11
hello this is your doctor's office calling with an important reminder we want to remind Holly that you have an appointment scheduled for Tuesday May twenty-fourth at nine thirty AM again your scheduled appointment time is Tuesday May twenty-fourth at nine thirty AM hello this is your doctor's office calling with an important reminder we want to remind Holly that you have an appointment scheduled for Tuesday May twenty-fourth at nine thirty AM again your scheduled appointment time is Tuesday May twenty-fourth at nine thirty AM

(800) 275-7387 // 5/25/11
hello this is a confirmation from 24PetWatch pet insurance program your policy has been printed and will be mailed within forty-eight hours of this call please allow fifteen business days for de-

livery please be advised that as a condition of insurance you are required to submit your pets complete medical history including doctor's notes to our office via fax e-mail or mail as indicated on your welcome letter document of insurance and policy terms and conditions

(800) 947-5096 // 5/25/11

this is an important message from AT&T to discuss your wireless service please return our call at one eight hundred nine four seven five zero nine six you may also access your account online www.att.com/mywireless again our number is one eight hundred nine four seven five zero nine six or six one one from your wireless phone thank you for using AT&T

Josh // 6/7/11

oh hi this is Josh um Div and I were just wondering if you and or Joey would like to get together later this evening uh for drinks movies or anything so uh give a call if you guys are interested be great to see you hope all is well and talk to you soon

Parents // 6/8/11

hi Holly this is Mom guess what I'm watching Hoarders and I thought you'd get a chuckle out of that and it's pretty overwhelming but I want you to know I really threw stuff out I I mean for me I was fairly you might say merciless anyway take care love you sweetie bye I did talk to Michael and we'll we'll have further conversations and we'll have a list of of must dos anyways so anyhow talk to you later love you bye bye

Joey // 6/8/11

oh hey it's me um just wanted to call and let you know that I got a text from my dad about the truck so I want to talk to you about it so give me a call when you get a chance love you baby bye

Joey // 6/8/11

you just called me come on alright call me back bye

LeRoy // 6/9/11

hi Holly it's LeRoy just wanted to confirm that your uh P-Queue proof is ready for your final view uh see you later

Joey // 6/9/11

hi it's me I just wanted to call and say that I was sorry I just wanted a chance to say hi um give me a call if you want I'll be here ok bye

Joey // 6/14/11

hey it's me I just wanted to call and see how the car went and stuff so um give me a call when you get a chance ok bye

Parents // 6/16/11

hi Holly I talked to um the director of our store and told her that I wanted off um the twenty-eighth of June through um July eleventh and she said that was fine although she did want me to work um one day each week but I definitely will have the eleventh off and I'll have the twenty-ninth off and um let's see um I'm not sure which day of the week the twenty-eighth is but um hopefully I'll have that day off I'll check with her again but I'm not quite sure what day she wanted me um to work but it's just one day a week which I thought was manageable if if you come to Seattle and um I'm thinking that um that's probably the best way we can get the best bang for our buck because if I go to Buffalo Dad's going to be disappointed because I think that it wouldn't be fair to him and um and you know um I just think that that this time around but I still want to go visit you in Buffalo so bad anyway I think this time around definitely plan on coming to Seattle so I'll talk to you later I'm at work on my lunch break and I only have a half hour lunch which is like over before I know it and I have about one minute before I have to put my apron on and go back down to work so I'll talk to you later ok love you sweetie bye

Parents // 6/17/11

hi Holly I'm finally calling you back uh it's Mom so give me a call when you get a chance ok love you sweetie yeah um so I bought ok

Joey // 6/21/11

hey it's me just wanted to see how it went with J and D um give me a call when you get a chance ok love you bye

Parents // 6/22/11

Holly give us a call and let us know how your test came out

Joey // 6/23/11

oh hi I don't know I was just thinking that I missed you and that it was stupid that I hadn't seen you um today so I wanted to come and see you but apparently you're off doing something so call me I miss you baby I love you ok bye

Joey // 6/23/11

hey it's me give me a call bye

Parents // 6/26/11

hi Holly it's Mom give us a call when you get a chance we love you we're looking forward to having you here Billy is getting his operation tomorrow morning um well we'll drop him off tomorrow um after seven thirty between seven thirty and eight and he's going to have this growth removed um from his eye so anyhow um you will see him post-operatively he'll be at the vet's all day tomorrow Monday and so um I'm hoping that we can hold off to buy the tickets together to go to Buffalo when you go back to Buffalo and then I if I'm going with you um um till you get here but if not give me let me know you know so we can do it right now Dad is off on a bike ride and I am washing laundry and I will see you pretty soon take care love you sweetie bye bye

(888) 587-0496 // 6/28/11

hello this is Orbitz TLC calling with a gate change alert Delta Airlines flight two five eight six has a gate change departure from Greater Buffalo International Airport is now estimated for six o'clock AM Eastern Time from gate twenty-three estimated arrival at New York JFKennedy International airport is seven thirty-five AM Eastern Time at gate twenty-five to hear this message again press one thanks for using Orbitz goodbye

[identifying information redacted] // 6/28/11

hello this is Erin calling from the Small Animal Hospital um calling to let you know we had received we had received Crayon's fecal results uh this morning and happily he is negative for any intestinal parasites any questions or concerns our number here is [identifying information redacted] um also if you haven't done so already still use the Profender that de-wormer that we did give you 'cause a lot of times the um uh fecal results can have a false negative um it comes out negative even though they might have parasites so still use that so uh definitely do that ok thank you very much bye bye

Joey // 7/1/11
hey baby it's me I'm heading to bed I'll be up for a little while I'm gonna watch something so give me a call I lover you ok bye

Evan // 7/2/11
hello Holly this is Evan um just calling to say hi and see how you're doing um would love to speak with you say hello and such uh so give a call back whenever miss you dearly hope you're well

Parents // 7/3/11
Holly the Katie Brown Workshop is on now anyway I'm sorry you can't answer the phone you can't see maybe it'll be on at three in the morning that will be six hours from now ok ok bye take care

Ellie // 7/4/11
hey holly it's Ellie um I ended up just going home like this afternoon because I kind of was like I thought you were going to Olympia I don't know if you ever did or not because I couldn't get all of your text message I only got something that said still up for it so um I anyways it was really good to see you and I hope you have a good Fourth of July give me a call soon and um we'll talk and um enjoy ok bye

Parents // 7/4/11
oh Holly I decided that that dress that I was gonna have Carolyn alter I decided I don't want it I decided I wouldn't wear it I I looked in the long mirror and it's just too much I mean I don't think there is any way that it can be redeemed so it would look you know ok so anyhow um talk to you later ok bye so you might as well return it that and the slip so I hope you I hope they'll let you return it and get some money back um bye bye I took you know the the ticket off of it and I don't think that I have the ticket at all so ok talk to you later bye bye love you sweetie

Joey // 7/5/11

hey it's me I just wanted to call and tell you I had my coffee and so I'm less of a grumplesiltskin if you want to talk sorry for being a grumplesiltskin give me a call ok I love you bye byes

Rachel // 7/5/11

hi Holly it's Rachel um I just wanted to call and say hello hope you're having a good time back home um my mom and I were talking and thinking that it might be fun for you guys to come over for dinner um Sunday 'cause I know you leave on Monday so if that works for you guys that would be awesome let me know or have well yeah let me know or give me a text or something ok 'cause I would love to see you ok love you bye

Parents // 7/10/11

hi Holly what date are we coming back um I mean what day am I coming back um what day and what time um my boss has scheduled me to work on Sunday but I wrote her a note saying it said that I'll be in New York on Sunday so um anyway I'm sure she can change it or whatever I mean you know whatever I'm certainly not I certainly can't change our travel plans um that's ridiculous anyway so I made it perfectly clear that I'd be out of town actually I said Sunday and Monday uh in other words the seventeenth and eighteenth but anyhow um when you get a chance give me a call bye

Brother // 7/10/11

hey little gangster it's your fucking brother so um uh give me a call when you get the message so I can know if you wanted to do something tonight or not because it's Sunday and sometimes I get to bed kind of early so anyways talk to you later bye

Brother // 7/11/11

yo bitch it's your brother call me back bye

Brother // 7/17/11

hey nigger this is your African-American brother seeing what your vajazz is doing how Mom's doing or whatever the hell peace out biatch bye

(888) 587-0496 // 7/18/11

gate fifteen estimated arrival at Seattle-Tacoma International Airport is ten thirty-eight AM local time at gate S five to hear this message again press one

Parents // 7/18/11

hi Holly here I am um and just to let you know that I am awake and I am ready for um the plane you know the um um when they have us uh get aboard the plane so they said boarding will be in uh let's see that would now be about um approximately now let's see about about fifteen minutes from now I'm completely ready I'm in sight of the area where you stand in line and guess what it's totally awesome they have um a concession stand there bye

Chris // 7/18/11

hey pretty lady it's me just calling to say hey and um you know try to talk to you my phone is still at my house I went to go pick up the car Chris is just sitting outside so I'm hanging out with him for a little bit and I'm going to go to my crib and get my phone and yada yada yada so I'll see you at three fifteen I lover you ok bye baby

Parents // 7/23/11

oh Holly I'm just I'm still bubbling from such a wonderful time I had with you and Joey I mean you guys were such wonderful I mean you know just how you planned things out and and I just I just everything we did was just it was so special so exciting and now I'm home I have my new heart monitor on Dad helped put it on yesterday I have to wear it for thirty days you know until it comes off August twentieth so I'll have to wear it all the time twenty-four seven um if I take a shower then it's off anyway uh that's the only time I take it off and anyhow so that's kind of you know it's a little bit stressful having knowing I've got this thing on anyway um I did go out and buy some bras so I'm wearing one of my new bras it feels good um anyway just missing you thinking about you and I'm so excited about everything that happened and it's sort of like everybody around me I mean you know they don't care but Dad does he's always interested in hearing what I have to say anyway talk to you later anyway you don't have to call but you know I know you need to have some time to have just you with Joey and just you by yourself too and you just all that and so don't let me interrupt that take care love you sweetie bye

Parents // 7/25/11

oh hi Holly it's Mom I'm just curious when you um you know got those um ordered those tickets for my return trip back to Seattle did you happen to ask if I could get a senior discount yeah I was it just kind of went through my head you probably did and um but anyhow oh dear too late now anyway but I don't know it just went through my head but you know me no biggie no biggie no biggie sorry to waste your time love you sweetie I had such a good time oh my god take care talk to you later

Parents // 7/25/11

hi Holly I'm trying to balance my bank statement and I um wrote down um that I had withdrawn uh in other words I took into account Orbitz uh Delta um seven four and then I did it again on seven eighteen I wrote minus two fourty-five forty-five to Delta Airlines Orbitz o-r-b-i-t-z um and I'm wondering I'm confused now whether I'm only supposed to subtract it once or if I was doing one of them for you or you know I'm just confused I just need to get it straightened out for my records anyway but I'm sorry to be such a drag anyway um I'll feel better when I get it figured out but um you know I know you can help me figure this out ok thanks take care love you sweetie bye

(661) 380-3000 // 7/27/11

hey it's me just calling you from Skype because I think I left my phone in the car uh just wanted to let you know that I sent out Elective Affinities and just seeing how you're doing ok love you bye

Parents // 7/27/11

hi Daughter I'm still trying to bask in the glow of the wonderful visit I had with you thinking about all the wonderful things um even including all the the massages you gave me so I could so I'd be so I'd be ok to get back on the plane I could make it for that I wouldn't feel I wouldn't not anyway you get the picture take care wondering how Joey is and how you are anyway love you sweetie yeah just had a day at work they re-paved the parking lot nothing new has happened here on this end take care love you sweetie

Al & Stella // 7/28/11
hey Holly this is Al hey I just wanted to see if uh you might want to come over tomorrow we're going to be loading our moving van um and we're trying to gather a crew at one thirty um we worked on it today we got pretty far but uh we just have a bunch more junk to carry around so um if you could do it just give us a call sometime in the morning ok bye bye

Joey // 8/3/11
hey it's me um I don't know I was just seeing if you could maybe give me a ride to Sweet_ness 7 if you were going to be done in time for that if not give me a call so ok I love you bye

Megan // 8/4/11
hey Holly this is Megan uh just calling to let you know I talked to your landlord he was super nice he said he'd send me a rental agreement he's going to uh increase the rent a bit due to the uh the new and fancy bathroom that's going to be happening so thanks again for the heads up and your help um and I'll probably be in touch soon hope you're having a good one bye

Josh // 8/5/11
hey Holly it's Josh uh it's a little after eleven just wanted to call and give you an update on when we're leaving um we probably won't leave right at twelve but I think twelve thirty is pretty reasonable so for us so give me a call or text when you get this just uh so we know that we can still be good to come pick you up see you soon bye

Parents // 8/7/11
hi Holly I got the prints and so I'll send you a set of prints and um anyway I'm looking forward to you receiving them ok I'll send them to the college I guess yeah I'll send them to the college let's see um or let me know um what's the best thing to do if I should wait till after you move although I'm dying to have you see them ok talk to you later bye love you

Parents // 8/9/11

oh just me Holly just calling to chat a little bit talk to you later love you sweetie bye

Jeremiah // 8/12/11

hey Holly it's Jeremiah um I am supposed to be talking to you about uh opening night um Chris had emailed and asked if I wanted to do it and I figured it's my turn anyway I was thinking um the one constraint that we haven't done yet in the last couple years is translation so maybe we could do a opening night uh you know translation as the theme and people could do all kinds of shit with that obviously um I'm thinking about calling it found in translation but I'm not sure if that's too cute for its own good um but I'm calling you because Steve told me that I should tell you the name of the title for the night by tonight so that you can uh work on the poster or whatever but I'm not sure that in the past there's even been a I don't think there usually is a title right you just put opening night and I'll send out an email that says what the theme is um so anyway um I don't think you have to have a title if you do then um you can you know use found in translation or just the word translation or whatever you feel like um ok so I think that takes care of it if you have any questions or anything just give me a call later

Parents // 8/14/11

hey

Parents // 8/14/11

oh Holly I just remembered that's what I was calling to ask what was the name of that funeral home but it's um I think I remember Amigone ok I think that's it ok I I wanted to tell Dad ok talk to you later bye

Tony // 8/19/11

uh Holly Tony [identifying information redacted] if you get a moment give me a call please [identifying information redacted] that's [identifying information redacted] thank you

Steven // 8/23/11

yes hi Holly it's Steve calling uh right about ten o'clock on a Tuesday um LeRoy sent an email and the proofs are in I will be down there in an hour uh so uh I'll be down there by eleven AM um I will go through them if you want to be there that's fine if not uh that's fine too uh but that is that's my plan and then I have to dash off and uh select cameras for the poetics archive with Scott uh ok hope things are well may see you in an hour down at um down at the printer's ok take care

Joey // 8/23/11
hey baby please call me back please ok bye

Jeremiah // 8/25/11
hey it's uh Jeremiah I am parked uh by your old building uh I'm kinda parked in two spaces that were open uh that you know close enough to the new place um and I think I'm parked in such a way that people can't get in behind me so it's kind of it's a big space I don't think it's big enough for the truck but anyway uh yeah call me tell me what you want me to do next uh I'll just be sitting here until then alright later

(800) 947-5096 // 8/26/11
This is an important message from AT&T to discuss your wireless service please return our call at one eight hundred nine four seven five zero nine six you may also access your account online at www.att.com/mywireless again our number is one eight hundred nine four seven five zero nine six or six one one from your wireless phone thank you for using AT&T

Jeremiah // 8/29/11
holly please call me back as soon as you get this message like uh as you soon as you hear my voice just call me back ok thanks

Parents // 8/29/11
oh Holly just curious uh where your apartment is from where your other apartment was um anyway um talk to you later love you oh such a sweetie take care bye bye I hope you have a great dinner tonight that you can sit down and enjoy it with Joey take care bye bye

[identifying information redacted] // 9/1/11
hi this message is for Holly this is the doctor's office calling you can pick up your prescription after two o'clock today the office will be open till six thank you

Unknown // 9/1/11
hello this is the gas company calling about [identifying information redacted] Avenue to turn the gas on please call six eight six six one two three to schedule for another day thank you

Joey // 9/5/11
hey it's me call me back ok bye

Joey // 9/5/11
hey what the fuck dude come on alright um so anyway will you listen to this the answer is bathroom from molding to molding is thirty-three and bedroom from molding to molding is thirty-five inches ok ok I love you goodbye

Parents // 9/5/11
hi Holly I just wanted to tell you um that your cousin is coming over tomorrow at six PM and so at some point we will try to do you up on Skype and so anyway some time if you get a chance give me a call and let me know if there is any good time you know for you like it would like your time it would be nine probably later between nine and twelve something like that so anyway so if you get a chance give us a call and so anyhow kind of exciting and she she is married and um so anyhow talk to you later love you sweetie bye

Parents // 9/6/11
Holly it's your dad your cousin will be here at six tonight that's Tuesday the sixth so be sure you're home she wants to meet you and see you on the on the Skype thing give a call and let me know you get the message otherwise I'm going to keep calling

Divya // 9/12/11
hey Holls it's Div I'm calling you because I assume Joey's phone is dead and that's why you called on your phone about his art materials um yeah we are happy to even drop it off tonight or one of you can come pick it up later on today we're just at home um doing

some work so give me a call and we can arrange a pick up or delivery service alright bye

Parents // 9/15/11

oh Holly let's see oh I was going to ask you this is Mom of course um you know I had had um it's called an overdraft account and it's like every time I get one they transfer it to you to your account I don't I don't know what's happening but so um I don't know you mentioned something about your financial aid coming through and um I don't know if there was just anything I'll talk to you later I'm in the doctor's office waiting for this damn doctor he uh oh my god it's just I am so disappointed uh ok remember I was wearing that thing for a month well they never gave me any real information on that so I waited the whole month they never they never gave me any information today I'm waiting to see the doctor and uh you know so maybe he'll tell me something more and I'm supposed to have this stress echo today and I thought that I was going to see the doctor after the stress echo no they scheduled me to see the doctor before the stress echo so that means that um that I'll have the stress echo I won't know the results of that I will leave here and um the whole thing makes me so upset I was so upset and I said things I shouldn't have to Dad and um I don't know I'm just I got upset about that and I got upset about the doctor thing and now my blood pressure's high and so anyway the nurse recorded a high blood pressure anyway I'm just having a low moment and I'll get over it today will tomorrow will be another day but anyway I'll talk to you later I'm just waiting for this doctor's appointment and and but if he doesn't even make it in time I won't even see him I'll just have the stress echo so this place here this hospital is you know just a big bureaucracy and I just feel like I don't matter at all to them anyway and um I don't know it's just it's too big of a bureaucracy thanks I'll talk to you later I'm sorry for being such a crybaby but I love you

Parents // 9/22/11

hi Holly love you sweetie oh I was going to tell you that there were fish that were about to lay their eggs and they were just um let me ask Dad where they were located at um it's just very very close to the cabin you could just look right down in the river and see them there was just like about twenty of them salmon and um Ed where was how do you describe where that the salmon were where they were about to lay their eggs ok up from the cabin about in other words closer to it than and they go ok they go all the way up to the next cabin right ok so uh so you know all the way almost from anyways there were fish in there just a whole bunch of salmon that were there bright red and they were about to lay their eggs there so that was really exciting to see that we saw one duck and on the road we saw two deer one was probably the female maybe a mother I don't know they were both one was real young it was real young the other one was young as well but not as young ha so they were Dad said they were both females anyway so I thought that was pretty exciting and and um anyway talk to you more about it later love you sweetie get some sleep ha sorry to call you so late love you bye

Jeremiah // 9/23/11
hey um it's me I thought I just missed a call from you maybe I just got a text or something I'm not sure yeah um yeah ok uh call me back I guess I haven't read your text I don't know what you want yeah but um I'll talk to you soon

Jeremiah // 9/24/11
hey uh it's Jeremiah you called me earlier and uh now I'm calling you back so call me back ok bye

Brother // 9/24/11
hey stinky it's your brother please call your brother back when it is convenient for you bye

Parents // 9/27/11
hi Holly I got the kitchen towels and I got a little desk calendar but it's mainly for the design the Frank Lloyd Wright stained glass window designs and I thought they might go ok bye

Parents // 9/27/11
hi Holly Dad told me you got the package I'm so happy anyway um give me a call when you get a chance love you sweetie bye bye

(866) 489-2669 // 10/8/11
hi this is Time Warner Cable calling with an automated survey regarding your recent experience with us we hope that you'll take

just a few moments to answer a five question survey if you are the person who interacted with our sales representative and are willing to provide this feedback please press one now

Todd // 10/13/11

hey it's Todd I hope it's still your number um it's been so long since I've left a message uh might be someone else's now I don't know anyway if this is Holly Melgard's number then this is a birthday message whooo happy birthday twenty-eight years old I think yeah you're twenty-eight I'm thirty that means you're twenty-eight um I wish you the best and I hope it's a good one um so uh you can call me back if you want if not I'll talk to you later bye

Katie // 10/13/11

hey I just wanted to wish you happy birthday um I wanted to put together a damn gina card um but I realized that that had some inappropriate contents to do at work and I'm still stuck at work so um anyway hope you're out doing something fun and hope I'll talk to you soon ok bye

Parents // 10/13/11

hi holly please um give me a call I wanted to wish you a happy birthday this is the first time I had a chance to call you I didn't want to call you early this morning because I thought you might be teaching I love you sweetie happy twenty-eighth many many hugs and kisses take care

Joey // 10/21/11

hey baby just calling to let you know I'm at C and T's I'm gonna have a couple of beers and then head home ok well I love you I hope you're sleeping alright bye

Parents // 10/25/11

hi Holly we played Skype um your recordings on Skype and they were amazing I was pretty much blown away and Benny was going berserk about the one where you were going no no no stay stay stay or whatever and the other one on pornography was amazing and you have so much expression and the way you handled the question and answer I mean I was boy it was amazing um anyway here's Dad so give us a call yeah you traumatized the dog thanks a lot

Parents // 10/25/11

Dad was trying to be funny however Benny was very very concerned we had to reassure him that everything was ok he he thought that his world was going to end as he knew it anyway give us a call

Adam // 10/27/11

hey Holly it's Adam calling uh I'm just with Kasey taking him to his hotel and we're sort of downtown it's at the Holiday Inn at Delaware um and yeah uh we were wondering maybe if anyone was hanging out tonight he was thinking maybe it'd be nice to get a drink with some people so so yeah give me a call if you get this and I'll try Joey as well bye

[identifying information redacted] // 10/29/11

hey fat ass this is your brother I'm calling you from my friend's phone but you can just call me back on my phone because I haven't paid my bill yet because there's a problem with it so I can get calls but I can't make calls so just call me on my phone and I'll tell you how gay you are bye

Parents // 10/31/11

hi Holly just called to say Happy Halloween and that I walked Billy around Green Lake with his sweater on and he's looking very dapper and I showed him off at PCC to a few customers few of the employees and um so he's just he was just a real trooper so that's my message I love you um um um we'll be in touch take care bye

Joey // 11/3/11

hey it's me also yes give me a call ok bye

Jeremiah // 11/3/11

hey it's Jeremiah I just noticed I uh I just missed a call from you I uh so uh uh yeah call me back if you need to alright later

Todd // 11/3/11

Smellgard I was just calling to see how you're doing I know you got uh well you got all kinds of PhD shit I don't even know what the fuck but I know you're hella busy and uh I just wanted to I just wanted to check in on you I don't know anyway um call me back bye

Joey // 11/5/11

hey babe it's me um just wanted to let you know the car is on Elmwood like directly in front of the house so ok I'll talk to you soon bye

Parents // 11/6/11

hi Holly just Mom just calling to say I love you I have to work today bummer talk to you later um don't get off until six thirty our time anyway have a good one um anyway hoping to just chat with you sometime love you sweetie bye

Parents // 11/6/11

hi Holly it's Mom um give me a call when you get a chance everything's fine uh I did see the cardiologist today and uh everything's ok but um I wanted to just tell you somewhat they're checking on now um ok so talk to you later everything's cool not to worry don't lose any sleep give me a call wanted to update you what's happening ok bye love you I um met with my new doctor now and uh I feel better um talk to you later bye

Parents // 11/8/11

yeah Holly it's your dad give us a call your mom wrecked the car again

[identifying information redacted] // 11/18/11

hello Holly it's [identifying information redacted] I was just calling you know about the essay and what I'm supposed to do regarding it being due on Monday you can call me back I'll probably be working but if you just leave me a message I can call you back next time I get a break alright

Parents // 11/18/11

have a good day call me when you get a chance

[identifying information redacted] // 11/20/11

hi Holly this is [identifying information redacted] from English class I'm so sorry I didn't call you yesterday I thought we were going to do the phone appointment Sunday um which is today but I looked at the note and it says Saturday so I'm so sorry I didn't call um just got confused about the days um if you want to give me a call back that'd be great I am at work till five but I will have my phone on me but then I have rehearsal five to eight and I won't so if you could call me before then or after that that would be wonderful um my number is [identifying information redacted] hope to hear from you soon thank you bye

Parents // 11/23/11

hi Holly thank you so much for telling us that you're about to board the plane thank you so much for calling to tell us that you're at the Detroit Airport and um we've been out all day obviously and I'm sorry that we weren't able to receive your phone call but anyway um we're going to the [identifying information redacted] tomorrow we're going to pick Michael up around three thirty and then um they said to be there at four so we'll be there about four and you know Carolyn she'll probably have the meal on a hell of a lot sooner than I would do anyway um I'm gonna fix a little um tofurky roast a little one and uh take it with me for Rachel we'll see how that goes over that way I get to taste it and she can have it whatever so anyhow I will talk to you later give us a call when you're at Joey's parent's place love you sweetie bye bye

Parents // 11/24/11

hi Holly um again we're sorry we weren't home to receive your calls about your um getting on the airplane and your being in the Detroit Airport and um but we just had stuff we had to do yesterday I had a doctor's appointment um and we were doing some shopping for Christmas a little bit had to pay a bill just a bunch of stuff I had to get some groceries pies for the [identifying information redacted] and um it just felt so good to hear that you were in those different spots and what was happening to you so uh give us a call when you get a chance I want to wish you a Happy Thanksgiving love you give us a call when you get a chance we're going to eat at the [identifying information redacted] at four o'clock so we'll be there to pick up Michael we'll pick up Michael at about three thirty and um love you sweetie bye I'm dying to know how it's going take care bye

Parents // 11/25/11

hi Holly give us a call if you get a chance thank you love you sweetie

Brother // 11/29/11

hey retard it's your brother get on your computer and look up Twinkle Toe Melgard Twinkle Toes Melgard on Youtube you can see me dancing it's really funny bye

Parents // 11/30/11

yeah Holly it's your dad uh give me a call will you when you get a chance it's nothing important

Parents // 12/3/11

hi Holly it's Mom the reason I'm calling is because um I know you were saying you get in on the twenty-first of um December um now I have to make a doctor's appointment at one o'clock and Dad could drop me off and then go pick you up or you know we'll work something out but um I just want to know what time you would arrive in Seattle so then he can you know be at the airport and pick you up and so um you know we you know we get you and uh I can also have my doctor's appointment I know we can get it to work out but um you may be coming in the night or early in the morning I I just have no idea so give me a call it's your mom love you dear anyway um Billy had his stitches out oh my god it is so long you should see oh my god I'll have to tell you how long it is you should see him oh little guy let's see the stitches are it's over an inch long little over an inch long yeah so he needs them on for about ten to fourteen days and then he's got one over his eye so anyhow he's taking it easy he's gotta be calm and stuff and oh poor little guy so anyhow yeah I just got home so anyhow I love you take care bye bye

Parents // 12/3/11

hi Holly um give us a call um I need to know when you are coming home when you'll be in Seattle um approximately on the twenty-first of December give us a call thanks love you sweetie bye

Chris // 12/5/11

hey it's me uh just wondering if I could get a ride with you guys tomorrow being Wednesday uh yeah give me a call back uh or I'll see if I can catch Joey online either way hopefully I'll see you in mañana

Parents // 12/8/11

hi Holly every time I think about your coming it cheers me up I don't know something about you just makes me feel more electric and alive inside take care and Joey too bye

Brother // 12/15/11

uh yeah hello this is uh Seamus from Weight Watchers yeah we got your application for membership and uh it looks like your credit card number didn't go through but we want to help you we're willing to donate our services for free and uh if you could give me a call back I think you have my number

Jeremiah // 12/20/11

hey uh Holly it's Jeremiah um uh let me know if you guys want to have a beer tonight I have a crap load of Pabst I bought for some reason and didn't use um so uh yeah uh give me a call you leave tomorrow I leave Thursday we should hang out before then ok later

(888) 587-0496 // 12/21/11

hello this is Orbitz calling with a travel alert here's the message hello this is Orbitz air traffic analyst Brian Wells calling with some delay information for your flight today the combination of low clouds and rain in Philadelphia Airport is limiting the number of aircraft that can land hourly as a result your flight may experience an average arrival delay of forty-five minutes please keep in mind that this will not change your scheduled check-in time thank you for choosing Orbitz we look forward to serving you again soon to hear this message again press one

(888) 587-0496 // 12/21/11

hello this is Orbitz TLC calling with your flight status update US Airways flight seventy-four is scheduled to depart Philadelphia International Airport on time at five fifty PM local time from gate B nine estimated arrival at Seattle-Tacoma International Airport is eight fifty-nine PM local time at gate A three to hear this message again press one

Parents // 12/21/11

Holly this is Mom calling from the cell phone um I believe you just tried to call um let me give you the number again [identifying information redacted] just call again I just didn't get to the phone in time take care

Jacob // 12/24/11
hey Boutros um Merry Christmas Jacob calling um yeah just calling to chat and catch up or whatever uh but I guess I'll try calling you back tomorrow um thank you for your mutant snowman as well um alright I guess I'll talk to you then alright take care bye

Parents // 1/1/12
hi Holly um give us a call when you know what's happening thank you bye

Ellie // 1/3/12
hey Holly it's Ellie just seeing what your ETA was I'm just about to leave my work right now so I'll be back home in like half hour um just give me a call alright bye bye

Parents // 1/7/12
Holly call us when you get a chance

Parents // 1/7/12
coffee's ready eight forty-one

Parents // 1/7/12
hi Holly um it's Mom guess what I did today I walked up to the mail-boxes mailbox place down the street and I wore the cowl that you made me and it felt so toasty and right now I'm nice and cozy inside um café um it's an espresso house that one that's near the post of-fice place on further down and uh I'm sitting in here with my coffee and I got a homemade biscotti with orange um candied orange in it made by the owners of the place um anyhow so I will share that with you when I get a chance and so I'm working on I I like to work on my bank stuff out of the house it just it just makes it easier to concentrate without Benny distracting me so I will talk to you later give us a call so I'm using the cell phone ok bye talk to you later

Parents // 1/9/12
just give us a call when you get there love you sweetie oh my gosh ok bye

Parents // 1/15/12

hi Holly it's Mom uh give me a call when you get a chance um take care love you sweetie bye

Chris // 1/17/12

Melgard it's me um I was just calling to say I got an email back from Divya she can't meet tonight she was hoping to meet tomorrow night which I'm fine with I'm just checking to see if you guys are ok with that it would be tomorrow night at your house at six so let me know and I will contact Div ok bye

Lewis // 1/17/12

Crayon Crayon I speak to Crayon I speak to Crayon

Parents // 1/20/12

oh Holly let's see I went to the bank yesterday and um the fellow at the bank the personal banking manager you know whatever at the bank said that um make sure that all your bank accounts are linked together with your bank that way you won't be charged the twenty or you should not be charged the twenty-five dollar fee per month per each account um the reason you don't ok so they send a letter and in the letter they say that if you don't have five thousand dollars in um linked accounts you know in any one of your like checking or savings in other words and if you are charged so you should check it each month and if you are you should you have to go in and protest but you may have to go into the bank to um get this straightened out so anyway give me a call if you have any questions about that they did send a letter saying that you have to have five thousand dollars in um one of your accounts um and so anyway 'cause they're trying to get by with this twenty-five dollars come on and uh you know so I just want to make sure they don't do it to you as well ok bye give me a call if you have any questions

Todd // 1/23/12

hey Holly it's Todd um so I got your message um you can call me back I've got the day off so you can call me back anytime um I was gonna call uh probably the Employment Office after I got off the phone with you so call me back and we'll get it figured out alright bye

[identifying information redacted]   //   1/23/12

hi this message is for Holly this is the doctor's office calling you can pick up your prescription after ten o'clock tomorrow morning we'll be open till six thank you

Parents   //   1/23/12

oh Holly I just had a little question to ask you uh when you get a chance um you know just call I have to work tomorrow from nine to five thirty so talk to you later love you sweetie bye hope things are going well thinking about you I saw Michelle today and I showed her the Christmas picture and she said you look adorable anyway she said you must be so proud of her and I thought of course I mean I shouldn't think of course I mean we're so proud of you ok love you bye bye

Parents   //   1/28/12

boop it's me Mom love you sweetie bye we had a great time take care want to tell you about it

Parents   //   1/29/12

hi Holly um I found the tapes and you had put them in um one of the drawers in that cabinet that's on the floor and I'm just glad I found 'em anyway and also that that pad for cleaning um mats and stuff anyway um now I guess I'm looking for some my metal um ruler long straight rulers anyway but um talk to you later love you sweetie bye

Parents   //   1/30/12

yeah Holly it's your dad your mom's in the hospital give us a call right away

Steven   //   2/2/12

Holly it is Steve calling you at three forty-five on Thursday I picked up the posters and the brochure they look fantastic and I also have your hard drive that you left at the uh printer's uh so whenever you want to get that back I have it at [identifying information redacted] I didn't want you to be worrying about that ok so hope to hear from you whenever ok take care

Parents // 2/6/12

hi Holly that was the woman that I had talked to previously from the doctor's office and she said that I sounded just fine and that um I sounded coherent to her and I apologized for sounding a bit gruff and uh she said that's ok she said just have a cup of tea you know relax and have a cup of tea and don't let anything bother you right now um and uh so the nurse will call tomorrow she wanted to call me to tell me the nurse will call me tomorrow and to just kind of rest assured and don't worry about anything and that's the most important thing ok so to take care of myself and not get upset about anything ok so I will talk to you later and I didn't press Dad he said that he would pay for that the dog's trip to the vet and stuff like that but I didn't want to pressure him or anything like that uh unduly because I just felt I need to rest and and he already told me that he would do it and so I trusted he will do it and um it's not a problem so I shall talk to you later have a good evening and don't worry about me I'm totally fine um um sometimes I almost wish you would worry about me I think you're more worried about the dog than me but anyway love you dear sweetie ok take care bye

Parents // 2/6/12

Holly I really would appreciate it if you'd call me I feel like I feel like you don't care about me I feel like you don't I I don't know I just you're hurting my feelings by not calling me please call me I don't think you understand I think you misunderstood what happened and I but besides from that I don't like the way you've left things it makes my feelings hurt I love you

Mechanic // 2/7/12

yeah I'm just calling to see if you've got your coffee cup

Parents // 2/10/12

yeah Holly it's your dad everything's a-ok so give me a call

Robbie // 2/17/12

hey Holly it's Robbie I'm just uh returning your call it's uh good to hear from you sorry it's taking like a week to get back to you um but yeah I'm doing well here and yeah it would be fun to catch up so just give me a call uh anytime ok bye

Jeremiah // 2/21/12

hey Holly it's me it's Jeremiah um I'm not sure uh what it is I'm try-
ing to say here hold on basically I was just calling because I'd like
to talk about this whole cover situation I just feel weird about sort
of the way it's going down like um I hate that we're talking about it
over email rather than face to face given that we're friends and um
I hate that uh it's become this sort of like um ultimatum between
your design concept and my I can't call it a design concept just a
cover idea or whatever it is um so I just feel like uh it would be bet-
ter if we just uh you know talked about it um and that I don't know
but it's less likely that way to like sort of you know to drive some
sort of wedge between us or whatever make us feel weird about it
um so yeah I'm at home reading uh if you have a minute sometime
today give me a call and uh let's talk about this situation um ok hope
you're well bye

Unknown // 2/24/12

this is [identifying information redacted] with a very important
message regarding your [identifying information redacted] debit
card we recently sent you a new debit card this call is to remind you
that your new card should be activated immediately upon receipt
to avoid any disruption of service to activate your new card please
follow the instructions on the front of the card if you have not re-
ceived your card or have any questions please call the number on
the back of your [identifying information redacted] debit card if you
have already activated your new card please disregard this message
thank you for being a valued customer

Parents // 2/24/12

hi Holly this is your mom uh give me a call when you get the mes-
sage love you sweetie I tried to transfer some money but I don't
know if the guy at the bank did it quite right or I may have screwed
up but I think we got it right ok thanks give me a call

Parents // 2/24/12

hi Holly um when you get home uh give me a call I want to make
sure that I didn't screw anything up I'll explain it to you later it's
no it's no biggie it's just that um I want to make sure I did the right
thing talk to you later ok please give me a call when you get a
chance love you sweetie

Parents // 2/25/12

um Holly if you get a chance could you please call me

Parents // 3/1/12

hi Holly just calling to say I love you thinking about you sweetie um three nurses came today oh my god talk to you later love you

Parents // 3/4/12

hi Holly it's just Mom telling you that um I'm feeling better and I'm in hopes that I'll get full recovery and um on Tuesday I'll be getting a CAT Scan and I'll see the doctor and um but you know this thing may take a little while but um I just want to give it a go that I'm going to do my best to recover from this damn thing ok take care so this is supposed to be a good message and make you happy I love you sweetie pie

Parents // 3/9/12

hi Holly it's Mom just calling to tell you that I put some of the money that I owe you for the bills you paid while I've been in the hospital in your I believe it's your account and um and I'll do the same thing next month ok I love you take care sweetie pie you're the best

Joey // 3/25/12

hey it's me just calling to see where you were if you were coming home tonight give me a call when you get a chance ok

Parents // 3/27/12

Holly we got the new rails in on the back porch and I think it looks good it looks industrial but it looks good it looks like a nice clean neat job so I can picture you on the back steps sitting there anyway smoking a cigarette oh god but anyway um I wish you could see it anyway um and what else there was something else I was going to tell you oh I saw a psychiatrist yesterday um I don't know if I'm going to go with him I'm going to check out another one tomorrow and um so I'm trying to find someone to monitor my medications and um anyway so that's some things that are happening here and Dad just got up from his nap and I love you sweetie you are the best daughter a mom and dad could ever have

Parents // 3/28/12

Holly tomorrow I plan to mail a box to you of three bags of Tim's Cascade Jalapeño chips a book on cats um you know cartoon type um that Dad thought you would like and um the other is kind of just a little surprise and if you don't want it you could give it to Tobin she might like it or you might want to keep it because it's kinda cute um anyhow um it kinda goes along the line of teeny tiny things teeny tiny miniature Japanese things I love you sweetie bye call me sometime

Parents // 3/28/12

oh Holly I just wanted to check I think your address is [identifying information redacted] Avenue Buffalo New York [identifying information redacted] could you just call to confirm that so I can send the package to the correct address I think the [identifying information redacted] address was the old apartment that you had that I went to um give me a call when you get a chance love you bye

Joey // 3/30/12

hey baby it's me um just calling we're getting back from TGI Fridays and um yeah just calling to say hey don't know how long I'm going to be up so I figured I would call well I'll talk to you soon love you babe bye

Joey // 3/31/12

hey it's me just checking and wanted to let you know I miss you and wish you were here yeah and I love you give me a call when you get a chance and I'll call you love you baby bye

Ellie // 4/1/12

hey Holly um hope you're doing well been thinking about you lately um wondering how you're doing I I the other day I was like is Holly just living and teaching in Buffalo I can't remember and like waiting for Joey to finish because I remember that you did finish so I don't know what's happening with you and I'm concerned so um I hope that all is well I hope that Joey's doing good and um yeah ok call me later bye

Parents // 4/3/12

Holly um could you try to reach Michael through your internet thing or whatever I've been calling him for about four or five days now and I have not received any you know there's he's not calling back not answering his phone I don't know if he lost his phone I don't know what his problem is but he's got a bunch of overdrafts from [identifying information redacted] I think Dad and I should just drive over to his place and see what the hell's going on um also there's been a debt collection agency it says this is a recorded message this is an attempt to um collect a debt and they give a phone number but they do it so fast I can't um I can't write it down fast enough and so it would either be for um Todd or Michael I did ask Michael about it he says he knows nothing about it you know Todd's the one that would be traveling around um anyway uh I've been sort of in the middle of working on taxes and I'm trying not to get stressed out over your brother so I'll go to an Al-Anon meeting tomorrow uh anyway I guess that's about it I love you sweetie and um don't get all stressed out about it and I know taxes are due the fifteenth so that's what I'm working on and blah blah blah anyway I love you Dad's had a terrible cold he's spent a lot of time sleeping um anyway so talk to you later love you sweetie

Parents // 4/10/12

hi Holly I um first of all I want to apologize for um I apologized to Dad excuse me hold on a second for calling him a fucking asshole so anyway we worked our way through the day and we were ok we made up we're being um positive about things again but anyway um hold on a second I wanted to tell you that the cat scan was really good it looks really really good and the doctor has ok'd me to return to work as of the nineteenth of this month which is in nine days and with no restrictions um you know use my best judgment as to you know what's too heavy to pick up and what's not but then I had the same thing when I had the hysterectomy and stuff like that anyway but anyways so um I got I had a lot of questions to ask the doctor it was his assistant who's also a doctor Doctor [identifying information redacted] is her name and I asked her lots of questions and she was very good and gave me very good answers she said I can return to doing exercises in the pool and that jumping up and down will not cause bleeding in the brain and that there will be no spontaneous more bleeding in the brain um you know unless of course I would fall or something like that which I will do everything in my power not to do and um Billy is well anyway Dad's doing a really good job giving medication it's like uh he uses like a syringe it's like a needle kind of thing and he squirts it in his mouth real fast funny how but he's really hunched over and his right paw he holds his right paw up so he doesn't step on it because it hurts and um anyway so he's not doing too well but um anyway we're just doing the best we can he did eat this morning and he's been he wants to go outside and uh but we're supposed to carry him down the stairs and um I'll let you go I love you sorry I was being such a bitch um I just uh um I decided I'm not going to bring up the thing about putting Billy to sleep at all I mean I actually I had not mentioned it at all yesterday and um you know I can think about it but but I don't I don't talk about it I'm leaving it completely up to Dad what happens with Billy so just wanted to let you know and uh talk to you later so love you sweetie

Myung // 4/11/12
Holly it's Myung could you give me a call when you have a second

Parents // 4/12/12
Holly I'm making a kind of chuckchucka I don't know how you pronounce it but anyway it has chicken onion red pepper and enchilada sauce in it and I'm going to do the fried eggs talk to you later your mom

Steven // 4/15/12
Holly it's Steve calling at about uh five past eight on Sunday evening um I'm wondering whether you got my response to the um posters that you designed uh earlier today um what I requested in that is that the actual date and venue be put in a position where it's more obvious um so uh I can't say much more than that so I'll be in all evening working away here and let me know how you are and how things are ok take care

Parents // 4/22/12
hi sweetheart Holly I love you um I just wanted to tell you um this is just a bit of trivia however on your part I suppose but I am reading a book that is so inspirational for me and it's the perfect thing for me to read right now after what I've gone through it's called My

Stroke of Insight by Jill Bolles Taylor PhD she's a brain scientist and her personal journey at the age of thirty-seven she has a debilitating stroke that um um effects her whole left hemisphere of her brain which is the one that where anyway she gives like a background of um and with little diagrams of the brain you know different parts you know left hemisphere what this controls that and blah blah blah all these different parts and then she goes through step by step she's thinking as she goes through the process of having a stroke and it's just fascinating um and and she's it takes her eight years to recover but she's just so incapacitated that she's like like an infant you know just like a newborn completely and it's just fascinating and I know you guys are too busy to read anything like this now you're completely involved in what you're doing but I could see how this um you know reading this could someday maybe when you're older whatever help you I mean it could help you with your concept of of reality and um anyway it's just fascinating I just wanted to tell you that I'm all psyched up about this and that's all that's it that's my bit of trivia and I love you have a good day take care anyway

Joey // 4/25/12
hey where are you give me a call you're making me nervous ok I love you baby bye

Parents // 4/30/12
hi Holly just Mom calling to say hi love you bye

Trisha // 5/13/12
call me back bitch it's Trisha bye

[identifying information redacted] // 5/19/12
what's up special ed this is your brother I was wondering if you knew of any good movies or something lately or whatever just give me a call back on my phone it's fucking up for some reason so I had to use my friend's phone to call you bye

Josh // 5/23/12
hey Holls it's Josh um I was calling to ask a favor of you and or Joey um Divya and I are planning a quick trip to Michigan to see my folks and we might leave tomorrow haha um and we might need some-body to look after our furry ones so if you guys might be able to

do that uh it would be I guess Friday Saturday Sunday Monday four days um give me a call back and just let me know if not if you guys are going anywhere or anything like that you know no big deal but yeah just give a call talk to you soon bye

Chris // 6/5/12
hi Holly it's me I just saw you called me earlier uh it's like three o'clock in the morning but I thought you and Joey may still be up oh never mind I'm answering your call now

Parents // 6/8/12
hi Holly this is Mom I was wondering if you got the package that the little package I sent you for what you requested um please give me a call when you get a chance I know you're really busy sorry love you sweetie bye

Parents // 6/11/12
hi Holly it's Mom anyway when you get a chance give me a call love you bye

Parents // 6/15/12
hi Holly it's Mom um let's see what it sounded like you said was hi parents Joey passed his I couldn't understand what the word was um maybe Dad can but in any case um anyway we want to congratulate him but first we want to know what we're congratulating him for um ok well we'll talk to you later um give us a call again talk to you later bye

Parents // 6/16/12
Holly this is Mom I found the Velveteen Rabbit if you get this message call me back if you're actually still interested in that ok it is now let's see just a second um our time nine thirty not quite five um give us a call if um that will help I don't know it's probably too late but um give me a call if you want bye

Parents // 6/16/12
oh this is Mom I just wanted to say that I really do hope that someone does record this um that it's something that they could keep and treasure um uh you know anyway so talk to you later love you sweetie

Jeremiah // 6/18/12

hey Holls it's Jeremiah I was just wondering what the plan is for Joey's birthday I realized today that it's uh the day after tomorrow I think um so uh yeah I just wanted to know what was the situation I know that we're going to see that movie but um I don't know what else anyway uh let me know ok hope you guys are well bye

Ellie // 6/20/12

hey Hollister how's it going um I'm just giving you a call back AJ said that you're gonna be in town in July which is awesome um so I'm pretty sure you were just calling about that but I'd love to talk to you just call alright bye bye

Eric // 6/20/12

hi Holly it's Eric [identifying information redacted] calling hope all's well um I just got a phone call from George he's uh doing some work down in the basement in your building and he said that there was a water leak coming um from it sounds like in your bathroom and I was just calling to see if uh maybe the shower curtain wasn't in the right spot or we had a potential leak on our hands that I should be looking at ah could you um uh you or Joe give me a shout back and we'll uh just kind of figure out if I should be heading over there um my number here is [identifying information redacted] thank you

Stella // 6/21/12

hi Holly it's Stella hi um I'm going to be talking to this Craigslist guy tomorrow morning like seven AM ha about when we can drive his car cross country and um I just kind of wanted to get in focus what you were thinking at this point about the trip um as best as you know so um call me back and um we'll be seeing you really soon ok bye

Parents // 6/21/12

Holly the blood not the blood test the test that I had guess what it was normal the mitral valve's normal and just a whole bunch of stuff is normal and there is a little bit of bleeding and regurgitation still happening in the brain but it's nothing significant so I just wanted to let you know 'cause I am so happy talk to you later love you sweetie pie

Steven // 7/4/12

Holly it is Steve calling you around eleven thirty in the morning um I got your e-mail but you still don't answer my question which is which is what time would you like us to show up tonight um that's the question that needs to be be answered ok hope to get some email from you later with an answer take care

Parents // 7/5/12

hi Holly this is Mom of course I won't talk because you're not there and you don't want to talk to me anyway but you're so busy um too busy for your mother just kidding anyway um I I just Dad said that you have a plan for the the bedbugs and just oh my gosh my little girl and the bedbugs and you're not a little girl anymore but anyway oh gosh I'm just wondering how you're doing with all that you know if that's I would be overwhelmed but needless to say but in any case I'm grateful that I don't have to deal with that anyway we put this stuff on the back of our dog's neck and it seems to be getting the flea situation under control I'm so fortunate I love you bye bye take care I'm crazy

Jeremiah // 7/10/12

hey Holly it's Jeremiah I just got home from the exam which of course I passed and though you know I'm not totally psyched about my performance but whatever I passed so who cares uh wait here you're calling me hold on

Stella // 7/11/12

hi Holly it's Stell I thought I'd just call you and say hi see how you were doing um ok talk to you in awhile hope you're ok and hope Joey's ok and um and everything's kinda moving along for you in a good way alright bye

Joey // 7/13/12

Holly please pick up

Parents // 7/15/12

hi Holly um I just wanted to confirm that yesterday I mailed some of the goodies as I had mentioned to you on the phone and the reason is because I want to cheer you guys up you need some cheer in your life and um I just um I don't know if this'll do the trick but um I just think that it can't hurt so anyway love you guys anyway I'm sitting in a coffee house and I thought it would be the yuppie way to go to look sophisticated and hold the cell phone in my hand and talk into it I'll talk to you later love you guys bye

[identifying information redacted] // 7/19/12
hi this message is for Holly this is the doctor's office calling you can pick up your prescription after three o'clock tomorrow the office will be open till six thank you

Eric // 7/19/12
hey Holly it's Eric calling it's Thursday evening around six o'clock just wanted to let you know I was here with the uh uh exterminator uh we were just going to see if we could take a walk through if you're home but it doesn't look like you are so um we'll do it for another time and I'll probably collect more information from you about um what you found recently here and pass it along to Tom and we'll go from there uh talk to you soon thank you

Joey // 7/19/12
dude you literally just called me so call me back um I don't know I love you and I miss you obviously if you don't have time to call me don't it's fine um yeah I was just making myself some pasta sauce so I didn't hear the phone ring sorry though love you babe ok bye

AJ // 7/27/12
hey Hollister it's AJ um sorry I didn't call you back this morning I'm still planning to get together tomorrow in the morning and and we should just proceed with the cabin plan Ellie got stuck with Lucas anyway this weekend so we can do Saturday night at our cabin and then um either stay all day or stay Sunday night give me a call back when you get a chance hope you're having a good day can't wait to see you tomorrow ok bye

(202) 769-0865 // 7/30/12
this was a political survey call we may call back later

(202) 769-0865 // 7/31/12
this was a political survey call we may call back later

Joey // 8/1/12

hey it's me just calling to say hi and say thank you for insisting on the conference call today I feel much better after we all talked and I love you and I miss you and I'm going now to pay your parking tickets because I realized that that has to be done and I don't want your car to get towed so um don't feel like you need to give me a call back I know you're hella busy right now so I just wanted to call you and say thank you for being somewhat understanding and for yes I was being out of control and thank you I love you and I will talk to you soon alright sweetheart bye

Joey // 8/1/12

hey baby it's me just calling to say hi um I paid our parking tickets that we had on your car they were four hundred and sixty four dollars which is crazy um and I'm not saying this to blame you or anything I just want you to know that that's taken care of um I love you and I miss you and I'll talk to you soon baby ok bye

(800) 689-9554 // 8/2/12

hi this is Carmen calling with Protect Your Home ADP Securities I was calling today in regards to reschedule your installation for the security system if you could please give me a call at one eight hundred six eight nine nine five five four again number is one eight hundred six eight nine nine five five four thank you and have a great day

(800) 523-3273 // 8/3/12

hello this is a check-in reminder from United Airlines we're calling to remind you that you can now check in online for your upcoming trip from Seattle-Tacoma on Saturday August fourth just go to united.com and use your confirmation number and last name to retrieve your booking thank you for choosing United Airlines goodbye

(800) 947-5096 // 8/4/12

this is an important message from AT&T to discuss your wireless service please return our call at one eight hundred nine four seven five zero nine six you may also access your account online at www.att.com/mywireless again our number is one eight hundred nine

four seven five zero nine six or six one one from your wireless
phone thank you for using AT&T

(800) 864-8331 // 8/4/12

we're calling to let you know that United flight forty-eight forty-
two from Newark Liberty International to Buffalo on Saturday Au-
gust fourth may experience delays the flight is currently scheduled
to depart Newark at four o'clock PM out of gate C as in Charlie one
one five and arrive into Buffalo at five thirty-three PM gates may
change so be sure to check the airport before departure it's impor-
tant to know that this is an estimated time and the flight actually
could leave earlier we apologize for any inconvenience thanks for
choosing United goodbye

(800) 864-8331 // 8/4/12

we're calling to let you know that United flight forty-eight forty-
two from Newark Liberty International to Buffalo on Saturday Au-
gust fourth may experience delays the flight is currently scheduled
to depart Newark at five thirty PM out of gate C as in charlie one
one five and arrive into Buffalo at seven oh three PM gates may
change so be sure to check the airport before departure it's impor-
tant to know that this is an estimated time and the flight actually
could leave earlier we apologize for any inconvenience thanks for
choosing United goodbye

Parents // 8/8/12

hi Holly it's your mom calling to say that we finished off the Bota
Box at our block watch party which was tonight and I'm sure glad I
could use a little needed a little bit of wine to relax me after work-
ing hard at work all day and then this block watch thing for which
I made a baby green salad with special hard boiled eggs um sliced
on top and avocado and turkey bacon and um grilled turkey breast
sliced real thin and um then I let people choose their dressing be-
tween bleu cheese or balsamic vinegar vinaigrette and I also took
what was left of some fruit salad that I made second batch of fruit
salad and what else Benny is getting into some stuff on the back
porch oh and I'm dying to know um what you and Joey think of the
chocolate the um the spicy or whatever the little bit of spice you
know hot stuff in the chocolate bars so let me know talk to you
later bye bye I know you're really busy bye love Mom

Parents // 8/11/12
hi Holly um let's see um I wanted to transfer more money into your checking to reimburse you but um I need to know uh I need to go over the account numbers so I'll talk to you later ok bye

Steven // 8/13/12
Holly it is Steve calling you at um ten past eleven on a Monday morning uh I have no idea where you are um whether you're on the west coast or back in Buffalo uh I'm phoning to let you know that the copy for the calendar is all ready and uh I you know at your first opportunity you could let me know um what the best uh time to get this to you uh I don't think there's any need to re-design um the calendar template we can use the uh one that you designed uh the last couple of terms so get back in touch with me either by email or or telephone if you do decide to phone it is area code [identifying information redacted] and hope you're both well take care

Parents // 8/13/12
hi Holly I put the money in your account as I said so um check it make sure it's there and um everything should be fine and I love you and I always love to hear from you take care sweetie pie what is Benny into now talk to you later bye bye

Chris // 8/13/12
Holly it's me I'm just calling to see if you got my text earlier about going to the drive-in uh please let me know if you guys are in and if you are if you want to ride with us 'cause we are more than happy to give you a ride like I said in my text we can smoke beforehand or if you're feeling brave enough maybe we could smoke at the drive-in anyways give me a call and I'll talk to you soon bye bye

Parents // 8/14/12
hi Holly Dad has a question he wants to um have you answer so um give Dad a call talk to you later love you sweetie bye

Parents // 8/16/12
Holly um the Netflix has been cancelled um could you pay it or call Dad and ask we were wondering if you could reinstate it you know um er or how we could start it up ourselves or anyway um anyway um give us a call I know you want to have some time off

sorry to bother you but you know I wish before you'd taken off you'd given me a call to let me know you wouldn't be available at all to be reached I mean sorry I love you don't feel I'm not trying to make you feel guilty it's just we've been trying to get a hold of you love you bye

[identifying information redacted]　//　8/22/12
hi this message is for Holly this is the doctor's office calling your prescription is ready for pick up will be ready for pick up I'm sorry after two o'clock today the office'll be open till six and eight till six the remainder of the week thank you

Parents　//　8/25/12
hi Holly it's Mom just calling to visit love you talk to you later bye

Parents　//　8/29/12
hi Holly it's Mom I wanted to tell you about something it's kind of a fact kind of thing it's not really a fact because I don't have my facts right uh Mark Twain invested heavily in a printing machine that would print where uh and this printing machine which was a new invention um it it would set it would supposedly automatically set type and it was called something like the printing typesetting compositor compositor was the word that was used in this machine and we saw a picture of it last night on television on this program about Mark Twain and it's the funniest looking thing you've ever seen it turned out that that invention was um a flop in other words the one that was invented um lost thousands of dollars for Mark Twain and was like a major thing in helping him to go bankrupt and um but and then there was an investor oh let's see a guy who um wanted to make it solvent and I think he was an oil um an oil baron or something and so he invested heavily in trying to make this invention work and um but it still they still couldn't make it work but anyway you should see this picture of it the word is something compositor but it's really kind of interesting because the idea was it would have parts that would set the type so the human being wouldn't have to set type as was the case in those days when this thing was invented anyway um so I'll talk to you later but I don't know if you could google it or something like that but just to see the thing with all the

different parts it's pretty amazing anyways talk to you later love you sweetie bye bye they also had a really good program on um about Will Rogers who was a very interesting character in American history very interesting the quotes from Will Rogers and um such as I've never met a man that I didn't like or some kind of quote like that but um anyway blah blah blah talk to you later love you

Joey // 8/30/12

oh my god you are missing right now the biggest Bieber in the world he's so sweet he's in the chair oh my god why are you not here and why haven't you texted or called me at any point tonight I miss you come home I hope you are buying chips if you're not will you please buy chips buy the chips buy some chips buy the chips buy chips snacks chips I want to eat them I'm not sober eat the chips ok goodbye

Parents // 9/1/12

hi Holly this is your mom uh give me a call when you get a chance let's see um I'm going to drop something for you today um we heard the most amazing story and um you've gone through the whole thing with bedbugs it's a story on This Is Your Life or Day in the Life or whatever the thing on Saturday morning on Public Radio is anyway so god oh geez love you sweetie um anyways I remember when you said we might have to throw out our couch well knock on wood so far we haven't had to but anyway talk to you later bye

Steve // 9/10/12

hey Holly it's Steve I'm calling to see what is up call me back when you get a chance bye

Myung // 9/11/12

Holly it's Myung um just wondering whether you have a copy of Judith's book Deathstar Ricochet I thought I had one I need it to plan some

Parents // 9/15/12

hi Holly guess what we went to the Puyallup Fair and had fun talk to you later give us a call we'll tell you about it bye you should see the hat that Dad got oh my god it's so cool talk to you later bye

Divya // 9/16/12

hey Holls Molls it's Div um I'm just calling to apologize because I don't think we can make dinner tonight um as much as we really really want to we have three deadlines this week that we have to make and the last two nights have all been taken up by poetry stuff and I don't see how I can like get through another weekend without work so we really really want to come but I the house is a mess and in shambles and our work schedule has been falling apart for the last week so I have to get things back on track and I'm sorry I have to flake out on dinner tonight I hope you guys have a great great time and uh send my love to Trisha and Josef and I'll see the rest of you very very soon ok bye

Parents // 9/16/12

hi Holly it's Mom I just wondered if you got your package um that I sent anyway um if you receive this call in the next say hour or so I'll give you the phone number the cell phone is [identifying information redacted] and um [identifying information redacted] so anyway um if you don't get this message then no biggie we'll be in touch talk to you later when I'm home bye love you

Parents // 10/6/12

hi Holly it's Mom calling to say hello and I love you I miss you give me a call some day when you get a chance love you bye bye

Joey // 10/6/12

hey it's me I didn't actually expect you to pick up I just want you when you check your voicemail to know that I love you tremendously and that you're the most important person to me in the world um yeah and that's it so I hope that makes you feel good when you check your voicemail and that's all I wanted it to do I love you baby I'll talk to you soon ok bye

Parents // 10/7/12

Holly guess what last night Dad and I watched a movie it's called uh A Serious Man yeah A Serious Man by Ethan and Joel Coen and guess who Joey looks like or guess who looks like Joey Ethan Coen not his nose but his chin and his lower lip and maybe his jaws um you know his cheekbones m'kay I just wanted to pass that on you gotta tell Joey that ok Ethan Coen not Joel it would be interesting if it was if Ethan's name was Joel then it would be like Joey talk to you later bye love you sweetie tell Joey hellobye

Steven // 10/8/12

Holly hi it's Steve calling you it's a quarter to one on a Monday I'm calling to let you know that the students scheduled to visit this Tuesday won't be coming for some reason probably something administrative on their end but in case you've organized anything and spoken to people if you could uh let them know this uh it would be appreciated and hope that New York is or has gone very well hope to see you around some time this week ok bye

Parents // 10/12/12

happy birthday give me a call love you bye happy birthday daughter I love you happy twenty-nine I love you bye sweetie

Parents // 10/13/12

hi Holly happy birthday um we took Benny to get his nails trimmed and um I got on the exercycle did my exercycle thing I'm almost finished with the book that I've been reading um the last one was um amazing anyway I'll tell you more later talk to you later sweetie bye bye have a good one happy birthday I'm so glad you're my daughter I'm so glad I had you thank you bye bye

Parents // 10/13/12

the sky ends at the beginning of the world it's a little funny when it gets uncurled by Holly Melgard infinity where the sky ends the big sky ends at the beginning of the sky it may be a little high but I can fly the sky ends big bang may it be a boomerang the sky

Chris // 10/13/12

hey it's me I'm just calling to see how tonight went and to see how you guys are doing and wish you happy birthday again don't call me back I'm going to bed but I'll talk to you tomorrow I hope everything is fun happy birthday bye

Steve // 10/14/12

hey uh I missed your call I guess we got disconnected I'll call back I'll try Joey too

Tobin // 10/16/12

Holls Molls it's Tobin um happy birthday and I just wanted to call to tell you that I am on the way to class right now I have class from seven to ten tonight so I don't know I don't think I'm going to be able to make it to your party because I still have work to do when I get home and I have to work in the morning and I don't know what to do but I really wish I could come you're calling me right now ok I'm going to hang up and answer

Parents // 10/21/22

Holly I am going to sing a song that I created when I was between eight and nine years old and um I thought I would sing it because it would let you and Joey have something to laugh about um it it before I sing it I want to say it shows my um naive uninformed patriotism um and remember I was a child and the country's very patriotic at the time so ok here it goes away up in the sky our flag will never die it proudly waves in the red white and blue as god watches over you you you ok I think I'll try it one more time no I can't do it one more time you guys can play that over and over again I thought you'd give it give you something to chuckle about love you guys hugs and kisses

Parents // 10/22/12

Holly um I just wanted to say um ask you if you and Joey are registered voters in the state of New York if you please vote we need your votes ok love you bye bye

Steve // 10/23/12

hey Holly it's Steve uh we are just checking to make sure that you um um are picking us up if you're not that's cool just let us know but um yeah that's it give me a call back when you get a chance

Parents // 10/30/12

hi Holly can you call Mom please Holly can you call Mom when you get a chance thank you bye I'll be at work tomorrow five to nine er nine to five

Liz // 10/30/12

hey Holly it's Liz um I just had a possibly good idea um not sure if it's a good idea I wanted to ask you if you'd be interested in writing something for this catalog uh e-catalog thing that we're making for this show um and I dunno give me a call when you get a chance and we can talk about it uh also um I'm going out tonight to see this friend of mine who's sort of kind of new in town so um maybe you could meet up with us and get a beer and uh he's cool you might like him ok give me a call back when you get a chance ok bye

Josh // 10/30/12
hey Holly it's Josh uh I'm so sorry to hear about both of your cars um I am out of school and in our neighborhood uh if you need or Joey needs a ride of anything tonight or tomorrow or whatever just give me a call let me know text me whatever so let me know if I can help hope you guys figure it out soon um it really sucks but I'll talk to you soon bye

Parents // 10/31/12
did you hang up bye

Macy // 11/2/12
hey what's going on um you called Allison Allison doesn't have any minutes on her antiquated caveman phone plan so I'm calling you back you should call me back alright

Parents // 11/6/12
Obama's our president he will continue to be our president thank god anyways I put cornstarch in my hair today it's been falling into my eyes all day but anyway I had to try your trick because my hair was dirty anyway um bye give us a call I'm so happy and and I think Inslee they're saying Inslee you know is likely to get it um instead of uh what's his name McKenna anyway so I hope that's the case anyway talk to you later bye

Parents // 11/7/12
oh Holly I have some good news um give me a call when you get a chance talk to you later love you sweetie bye

[identifying information redacted] // 11/8/12
hello this is your doctor's office calling with an important reminder we want to remind Holly that you have an appointment scheduled for Monday November twelfth at nine fifteen AM again your sched-

uled appointment time is Monday November twelfth at nine fifteen AM hello this is your doctor's office calling with an important reminder we want to remind Holly that you have an appointment scheduled for Monday November twelfth at nine fifteen AM again your scheduled appointment time is Monday November twelfth at nine fifteen AM

Parents // 11/10/12

hi Holly I'm sending some more stuff in the mail talk to you later give me a call when you get a chance

Chris // 11/11/12

hey smelly you're probably still asleep I was just calling about the cat uh I just wanted to make sure about what time you guys were going to be home tomorrow so I can properly uh properly schedule the rest of my visits to Crayoid um I'm here now I didn't get here early this morning so um yeah anyway give me a call back I'll talk to you later bye

Leonard // 11/24/12

hi Holly it's Leonard calling just got back to Olympia I was in New York I had the feeling that you were in Buffalo and not in New York although I know you're uh curating things in New York these days but um anyhow that's why some of my messages were brief I was running around a bit much but on the flight back I read the whole the whole Hardt transcript it seems great it sounds just great and uh and I think it um looks good so I sent it on to to Michael to proofread and see if he has any changes he wants to make and I assume he'll send it back to me shortly and I'll send it on to Andy [identifying information redacted] and that's it for uh for their December issue so really the only timing issue then is at least what I can see is pulling the three interviews together as uh as a book um and um that would come sometime after December since he wants to run the interview in December and then sometime after that put the whole eBook up there so that means that the only outstanding issue as near as I can see is the introduction which you'll be writing and um um doing what you want with it but I can see three elements to it um which is uh at least four elements writing about the transcription process writing about Hardt's um overall philosophical prospective um certainly I'd appreciate it if a lot of the questions come out of mine my poetics there could be something on on um my poetics in that introduction of course something about your poetics work you're doing in your occupations pre-occupations uh trajectories and so on should go into that introduction too I think so so I think that's what I see as the complex but um worthwhile task ahead and maybe we can still I think I emailed saying maybe we could speak Sunday I have a little time today after I get a little nap in but uh if we wanted we should further and maybe find a time tomorrow I'm at [identifying information redacted] hope you had a good Thanksgiving and see you soon by the way will you be in um Olympia or Washington or Seattle in early January if you are it would be fun if you had time to visit my class but I don't know if Seattle fits in your plans during uh just after Christmas time or not but we'll speak a little later ok bye bye

Parents // 11/25/12

hi Holly it's Mom I haven't um I am afraid that I we may have missed Joey's parents um I wanted to meet them and yesterday I had to work all day I came home just exhausted and I asked your father if I should if we should you know call and Skype you know and he said no he had to eat right then because of the diabetes anyway so I fixed dinner by the time I did that I was just I was just wiped out and it was very late and um anyhow right now I'm just really tired I've got some kind of cold and it gives me a sore throat and really tired and I have to work tomorrow from seven in the morning until four I have to prep I have to start prepping for um this colonoscopy and um I have to even start start in on it at work I couldn't get out of work my boss wouldn't let me off um anyway um so then on Monday at one thirty I'm supposed to be at the gastroenterologist and have the colonoscopy uh which is a routine thing but it's always a good idea to see you know how everything's going on anyway well I'll let you go talk to you later love you and I wanted to meet um Joey's parents and it's so good to talk to Joey and it's so good to hear you're happy with them and that you guys are having a good time it made me so happy to know that talk to you later love you sweetie bye we had a good time too we really did um enjoyed talking with Michael's girlfriend it was just uh and Dad enjoyed the meal Dad was a lot of fun and we all enjoyed and laughed at dinner and it was just really good times good feelings and talk to you later tell you more about it and love you sweetie bye bye

Parents // 11/25/12

hi Holly it's Mom call when you get a chance there's nothing wrong it's just that I am going to have a colonoscopy and I want to hear your voice I'm going to have the colonoscopy tomorrow at one thirty PM and I have to do all the prep which is a pain in the ass anyway so um I'm not looking forward to this night of multiple trips to the bathroom very very annoying I'm just really pissed and I hate it I hate it I hate it I hate it I had to work all day too talk to you later bye

Parents // 12/3/12

yeah Holly it's your father give us a call and be sure to bring The Reader back when you come the movie the DVD bye

Parents // 12/7/12

hi Holly guess what you'll have to call me to find out what talk to you later bye love you

Parents // 12/10/12

hi Holly it's Mom I have a question ok I have a choice of buying the um salmon the smoked salmon for Joey's parents um now at Bartell's but at my work for fifteen ninety-nine they have a beautiful box it has this metal part with a carving of a Northwest Indian design and wood on it and it has eight ounces of smoked salmon in it and it would be a beautiful gift um that and it's not a whole lot of salmon but you know you get this beautiful box with it and then the coffee what do you think of that idea or um I could get one or two boxes of salmon at my store now in that box is not king salmon but um it just says smoked salmon generic smoked salmon whatever that is anyways my store has the same brand it's potlatch or something like that and um they have king salmon for um I think it's like twelve ninety-nine and then they have um keta salmon I don't even know what that is they have a trio for like twenty-three or maybe more than that twenty-six ninety-nine that is pretty pricey but it has a trio of different kinds of smoked salmon but that's almost about thirty dollars and um plus the coffee and shipping and whatever then I need to get um Joey's parent's address so um these are questions I have I work tomorrow from seven to four and I would like to whatever I get I'd like to get it on Wednesday and mail it on Wednesday which is day after tomorrow ok and guess what I'm making a fruit cake Dad has been wanting a fruit cake forever and I'm finally making it and I'm using cognac instead of brandy and I'm having cognac I'm drinking a little sipping tell Joey Mom's sipping a little cognac while she's making the um with the cognac I thought it had it calls for um let's see it calls for five ounces of dried figs and I thought I bought dried figs but it turns out they're Turkish apricots dried apricots but anyway I chopped them up and I soaked them in three tablespoons of brandy and then I let's see have like a half a cup of raisins golden raisins and I soaked those in brandy the recipe didn't call for it and then let's see what else I have let's see it called for um candied cherries and um I'm substituting some of those for um natural pineapple and I'm soaking that in brandy with some of the cherries candied cherries and oh my god it's so good it calls for four eggs and um flour and on and on and all these delicious things and oh my god it is so good brown sugar cup and a half of brown sugar cup and a half of flour and four eggs and blah blah blah love you give me a call if you get a chance if you hear this before you go to sleep tonight otherwise I will hear from you tomorrow

Parents // 12/15/12

Holly bring The Reader don't forget your father

Parents // 12/23/12

hi Holly I think it's going to be about twenty minutes fifteen minutes before um um we're it's our turn for with Santa fifteen twenty minutes twenty minutes that the most I'm thinking that's what I'm guessing

Joey // 12/26/12

hey it's me I wanted to say that I'm sorry and it's totally my fault I should have focused on how like blown away my parents were by what you sent and everyone was they were very very touched um they thought it was the sweetest thing in the world and I want you to know that I love you and I want to spend my life with you and I keep saying that because I mean it and yeah I've been thinking about you and talking about you a lot and I'm sorry ok I love you baby

Parents // 12/24/12

Holly guess what Jo [identifying information redacted] has a glass pie plate that she can lend us ok I've given her lots of cakes and things like that and stuff I've made for her and she would be happy to do that so I hope you get this message ok I don't want you to have to spend the rest of your night running around trying to find a damn glass pie plate I know how important this is to you please pick up the phone bye love you Mom it's about thirteen minutes to eight now

Kate // 12/26/12

hey girl it's Kate um just calling to see if you're home for the holidays I'm in Seattle and thought maybe you were here so um regardless give me a call back I'd love to see how you're doing and have a good day talk to you later bye bye

Ellie // 1/1/13

hey dude how are you happy New Year just wanted to call and say what's up and see how you're doing um give me a call when you get a chance I hope um that you guys are doing well and um yeah best wishes for twenty thirteen ok bye

Parents // 1/13/13

hi daughter I'm at Caffe Fiore and I'm going to be quick sorry the Seahawks didn't win anyway talk to you later I got Michael um a desk calendar it's um the car talk guys doing car talk anyone one you know one different thing for every day of the year and I also got him a little desktop thing not that he needs two but they were on sale half off um excuse me anyway the second is um has guitars fender guitars different kinds different ways their painted and stuff like that and I thought he'd enjoy that but anyhow um talk to you later love you Dad's having oh Dad's having surgery tomorrow um no not tomorrow excuse me Tuesday Tuesday we have to be there I think it's at fifteen minutes to seven I think that's what time we have to be at Northwest Hospital it's gonna be at Northwest Hospital and it's probably a day surgery but um you know if they feel he needs they'll keep him overnight for observation so anyhow um give Dad a call and talk to him and give him a pep talk and all that jazz so he's in a pretty good frame of mind and he's the one that elected to have this done and it's a good thing it's it's something that needs to be done and he's a really good patient so I will talk to you later love you bye bye

Parents // 1/19/13

hi Holly this is Mom um I'm going to the bank and I was going to transfer three hundred dollars more into your account for the bills you paid and I want to make sure it's the right account um you can call me on my cell phone yeah ok so yeah I want to make sure I get it in the account I want to transfer three hundred dollars so I hope you can call me back love you bye

Trisha // 1/28/13

hey Holls it's Trisha um the boys just called me and said they're having some trouble with the recorder because they connected it to the computer and it didn't show up on its own so if you wanna give them a call if you get the chance because I don't think I could help them um or just call me back and let me know what you think and I'll give them a call thanks sweetie hope you're doing well bye

Brother // 1/31/13

hey it's Mike we just wanted to know where Holly New York was and if you knew where it was that's all you're probably asleep so don't worry about it you can call me back tomorrow or never bye

Parents // 2/7/13

hi Holly just calling to say I did some drawings today and I feel kinda good about some of 'em I kinda did the little break ground breaking things just a teeny bit you know progress is always so but anyway and ah it feels good so right now I'm so tired gotta fix dinner for Dad but it's easy it's going to be warmed over Chinese food from our favorite Chinese restaurant talk to you later oh bye the way I have a real easy recipe to make it's something very very delicious and I wanted to tell you about it it's super easy and um I'll tell you it's a vegetable dish talk to you later bye love you

Chris // 2/10/13

hi Holly it's me sorry I trolled you so hard yesterday you were just trying my limits and I had to strike back um yeah so I'm just at the cafe I was calling someone to tell them I basically finished my prospectus so I am just getting drunk and partying um call me back hopefully maybe I'll see you guys tonight I would like to let me know ok I'll talk to you soon bye

Parents // 2/14/13

oh Holly I've got the I invented the neatest recipe ok you take pasta especially angel hair or fine spaghetti you know noodles ok and you cook them until they are just barely al dente just barely then you drain 'em don't rinse just drain and then you take in the meantime you're shredding at a fine shred um a zucchini a small zucchini and you also have on hand shredded um romano or you can do par-mesan but romano something with some bite to it like romano or a-s-i-a-g-i-o cheese and you take some of that and you throw that in anyway you throw these into the pasta and some oil and oh my god the zucchini is so good with the pasta and the but anyway in the pasta I always use salt and I always use a little bit of olive oil and um anyway so I just wanted to tell you about that it's so good talk to you later bye love you

Parents // 2/18/13

hi Holly um I have some jokes that I wanted to deliver to you ok some verbal jokes that I wanted to get your opinion on because I thought they were very they were thought-provoking and one of them is for Joey no actually both of them both of them are for you and Joey and there's more than two there's a whole bunch ok talk to you later love you bye bye it's your mother

Parents // 2/19/13

oh Holly I'm reading this joke book and I'm going berserk there's so many funny things in it oh my god I'm going crazy anyway um let's see if I can find one I don't know it's just oh my god um why is it why is it called tourist season if we can't shoot them let's see ok why is brassiere singular and panties plural let's see oh there's all kinds I'm just going crazy anyway talk to you later um ok I love you bye bye

Parents // 2/22/13

hi Holly I finished transferring the rest of the money into your ac-count love you sweetie bye talk to you later bye give me a call when you get a chance

Brother // 2/25/13

what's up nigger I'm just trying to get my voicemails published just kidding I'm just saying hi nothing important or urgent or anything just give me a call when it's convenient bye

Parents // 2/26/13

oh Holly I just wanted to tell you that I'm watching a show it's on Channel 9 it's called uh Women Who Have Made America and they have Gloria Steinam who's the founder of um Ms. Magazine and another woman who's co-founder of Ms. Magazine um and as well as all other kinds of women blah blah blah

Parents // 3/1/13

hi Holly it's Mom um sometime Dad's sleeping now but sometime when you have time give him a call he'd love to hear from you ok that's all not saying another word love you everything's fine take care bye Mom

Steven // 3/2/13

Holly it's Steve calling at five past two on Saturday uh I am trying to get Joey's cell phone number the one that I have on the grad student list is not working anymore so if you could get him to text me the phone number or if you could do it it would be appreciated ok bye for now

Frannie // 3/2/13

hey lady this is Fran when you get a chance give me a ring back bi-atch bye

Parents // 3/7/13

hey Holly tomorrow we will be married forty-four years so anyhow um love you dear thank you bye bye talk to you later Dad's doing well and I need to cut his hair tomorrow and we'll go out to dinner some place different if you have any ideas give us a call love you sweetie bye guess what the model that I drew at Gage today anyway he writes poetry and I um told him that you go to the University of New York at Buffalo and he said that's where he went anyhow talk about a small world anyway he said it used to be an excellent you know it used to have an excellent program the state poured a lot of money into it way back when he went there I guess anyway whatever blah blah blah talk to you later give me a call bye so I gave him your name and he's going to look up your webpage oh and by the way the drawing that I did of him he's posted it on his Facebook page and he's had a lot of really positive comments about it talk to you later bye

Brother // 3/9/13
hola it's your brola so give me a calla niggala peace

Katie // 3/10/13
hey I was just thinking about you and I thought I'd try giving you a call so I hope things are going well and I know you're busy so you probably won't call me back hahaha but um maybe I'll touch base with you sometime soon ok bye

Parents // 3/12/13
oh it's just me Mom um question have you ever heard of Meredith Monk I believe she was in Eastern New York anyway she's a composer singer director choreographer filmmaker and artist anyway we watched a documentary on her by um Babette Van Loo v-a-n-l-o-o anyway it was kind of interesting it was curious talk to you later love you sweetie bye

Frannie // 3/22/13
Holls it's Fran I don't know if you headed out of town for the weekend or what but anyhow um I just felt compelled to call you and I will answer your call if you get a chance to call me back I'm sorry I've been flaky about it but anyways I would like to talk to you and uh if you get a chance to give me a ring back that would be fabulous otherwise you can just hit me up on Facebook alright mamacita love you talk to you soon bye

[identifying information redacted] // 3/24/13
hi Miss Melgard it's uh [identifying information redacted] I'm just wondering about my submission so right now for each page I should just put my full name and page number like page one page two for each page at the top um left aligned and um I just send do I send them all to [identifying information redacted] email in PDF and DOC forms um I that's all the questions I have so far ok thank you much goodnight bye

(616) 613-2100 // 4/1/13
to the financial stimulus so press one now to take advantage today

Nick U // 4/3/13
hey Holl it's Nick uh yeah I was just calling because I hadn't talked to you in awhile and I wanted to see what you thought about the book too I have to say I thought it was pretty cool I'm glad you liked it um just seemed like perfectly made for you anyway this is my new phone number it's actually Google but it forwards to my mobile too ok hope you're doing well

[identifying information redacted] // 4/5/13
hello this is the office of Doctor [identifying information redacted] calling to remind you of your upcoming appointment please bring your updated insurance card your appointment is at our Amherst office the appointment is for Holly on Wednesday April tenth at eleven AM if you have any questions or are unable to honor this appointment please contact us at our office thanks and we look forward to seeing you

Parents // 4/6/13
hi Holly um give me a call I have to work tomorrow anyway I work from um nine to six o'clock but um anyway I'm starting taxes uh I'm wondering if you how you're doing on that anyway love you take care miss you tired talk to you later wondering how things are going with you always like to hear what's up take care bye

Parents // 4/8/13
hi Holly just Mom just to tell you that your birthday is the same day hi just to tell you that your birthday is the same day as Margaret Thatcher's birthday um miss you

Parents // 4/12/13
hi Holly it's your mom um let's see I just wanted to tell you that on our taxes because we file you know all this complex stuff um that all I have to do is the medical so I hope you're I hope that your taxes are you know you're being able to work on them and getting that taken care of anyway I love you Billy's been um you know he's oh gosh he almost haha anyway what should I say he's having more difficulty walking and he um is kind of leaning and kind of falling a little bit over he's walking up the steps the basement steps today

anyways in-between the dryer and well it's on the steps but um he fell to the right and what caught him falling through was the dryer but if his ribcage was thinner he would have fallen all the way to the floor and it scared me and I got him up but man he's starting to have real difficulty walking so I'll talk to you later poor little guy he's so thin anyway love you sweetie bye bye

Parents // 4/16/13

hi Holly well I went through an excruciating thing yesterday um I'll tell you about it when when you call but um anyway talked to an accountant today and um it should get straightened out but I'll have to tell you what I went through and uh I wanted to know it had to do with the tax thing and going to [identifying information redacted] and anyway uh anyway um and the preparer said you owe the government like forty-five percent of our income or some kind of thing like that and I just and I just went into shock anyway I wanted to know how your tax thing you know how things are going on that and I wanted to tell you more about my experience and um anyway so I love you dear and um I was talking to a mom today and she had a daughter I said isn't it wonderful having a daughter it's so nice so anyway love you sweetie give me a call when you get a chance bye oh by the way why doesn't this is for Joey too why doesn't the Dali Lama vacuum underneath his bed because he doesn't have any attachments talk to you later oh by way oh I'll tell you another one when I talk to you on the phone anyway bye love you

Parents // 4/19/13

Holly they caught those guys you probably know that but we're so pleased about where things are at right now and um I'll talk to you later anyway I told you the joke before and I'll tell you one more time why did the Dalai Lama not vacuum underneath his bed he had no attachments love Mom talk to you later that was for Joey anyway he'll hate me for it he'll say I'll never want that woman to be my mother-in-law for god's sake anyways are you going to run all these jokes maybe you could do a poem of them a collection including repeats I'll talk to you later bye bye

[identifying information redacted] // 4/23/13

hi this message is for Holly this is the doctor's office calling you can pick up your prescription after eleven o'clock tomorrow the office will be open till six and eight till six the remainder of the week thank you

Amanda // 4/23/13
hey friend I'm calling because I wanted to talk to you about this whole hiring thing ugh there was just like a bunch of stuff that happened today um that I wanted to talk to you about on the phone instead of like you know via email or something um we wrote a whole response to all of your questions um because the meeting yesterday was just ridiculous and then there was all this departmental drama in terms of um the Poetics people sort of alienating themselves or it's kind of a long story so anyway sorry I'm walking to my car so that's why I sound out of breath but um if you have any time tonight give me a call or otherwise um we could talk tomorrow or something um I just wanted to kind of give you the skinny and let you know what's going on ok talk to you soon hope you're well bye

Josh // 5/4/13
hey Holls it's Josh um I just had a quick question for you if you get this uh could you just give me a call back uh thanks

Joey's Dad // 5/9/13
Holly this is Joey's Dad would you do me a favor and have him call us call me sometime today I would really appreciate it thank you

Parents // 5/10/13
Hi Holly give me a call when you get a chance anyway I wanted to tell you about a poem I heard on public radio that was really cool it was um it was a letter to Mick Jagger by the St. Paul Chapter of the Daughters of Norway and um it was it was just very hilarious and uh I have the name of the person who wrote it and if you could find that and also there's a book it's called let's see Advanced um Clothing or something by this woman Ariel or Ari her last name's Cohen she is an older woman she's very stylish a fashion designer and the photographs of older women you know with really knock out um you know clothes clothing combinations that they put together you know just really out there so cool uh it's a book that came out and I would love if you I don't know if there's a way you can google what it is it's Advanced Fashion or Advanced I forgot the last word I should have wrote it down haha it's two words Ad-

vanced something or other and it's all these older women just some are like Barbara [identifying information redacted] and they're just really out there it's such a kick looking through that anyway and I wanted you to see if you could see what that looks like anyway I'll talk to you later bye love you sweetie give me a call Mom ok and guess what Michael is applying for a job I think he might get it and it would be a good job for him it's painting cars and it's in the neighborhood and um I I think he's gonna get it but it's going to take time to find out he's got the interview uh it's coming up this next week so talk to you later and I'm so pumped about those girls that were held captive for ten years their release and um I'm just all pumped about that I'm just it makes me so happy I think that anybody who's a survivor of childhood sexual abuse um and because I fall into that category I really really feel that this is so wonderful you know from my very gut I'm just happy happy happy talk to you later love you sweetie bye

Parents // 5/15/13
hi Holly I miss you give me a call sometime when you're not too busy to talk to your mom love you take care love you

[identifying information redacted] // 5/16/13
hey Holly this is [identifying information redacted] calling again I'm sorry to bother you but I've been thinking like really hard about this and like some reason like I know you have to like save yourself with the grades or whatever but like a B to me for some reason isn't settling well I worked really really hard in your class you keep telling me that my work was exceptional like I got hundreds on both portfolios like my participation was a hundred as well and for some reason it just doesn't sound right like I know it's not fair to give me an A or anything but like I don't know if there's a way that I could possibly get a B+ if that's possible um I just know that I really did work hard especially with the cards that were dealt to me this semester with what's happened and and I don't know if any way that can be reconsidered again um call me back if you have to or if not then I guess I'll just see what happens when the grades come out tomorrow

Parents // 5/19/13

oh Holly as it stands now my boss said that yes um I that week before the last week in June uh would be ok but she said as soon as I know to write it to write it in the special request book but anyhow so I do think that the weather unless it's too soon to do tickets or whatever you know and you want to wait we can always do that so there's always these options there's the option of possibly June and then there's possibly the option of August or maybe in July depending on what happens um but I do know that as the weather gets hotter it probably would be more difficult for Dad he probably would be more uncomfortable for sure but then just keep that in mind and that doesn't have to be the case I know if he anyway he's all pumped he's getting excited and oh my god anyway I'll talk to you later when you get a chance as soon as you know let me know ok love you

Parents // 5/20/13

Holly give me a call when you get a chance bye

Parents // 5/21/13

hi Holly I wrote in the special request book for work that I want to have the second week before the end of June off in other words the fifteenth or sixteenth through the twenty-second off um I may have to change that but anyway in case Dad can come during that time um anyway I still can kind of change it I think I'm entitled to two weeks off in the summer maybe even three but two anyway but I know that I'm gonna I'm gonna really need to have some time off from work during that time and my reason that I'm going to take time off is if Dad's gone someone needs to be in the house to let Billy in and out his kennel every two and a half hours two and half to three and a half hours at the most um and what else please give us a call ok I know you're busy but we need to hear from you ok take care love you bye I hope you're feeling better love you

Parents // 5/22/13

hi Holly this is your mom again this is something I wanted to tell you and have you on the other end and not your answering machine but um let's see what was it the day before yesterday guess who said hello to me at work Thomas remember Thomas from Olympia and Meredith was there as well and uh it just felt so good it felt so good to see him and um he looks he looks good you know he's growing in he's not such a boy anyway but it was good to see him I just wanted to share that with you and the other thing is I want you to have Joey call me or I want to tell him a joke maybe I'll just tell it right here Joey ok Joey are you listening this is very important what is brown and lives in the bell tower the lunch bag of Notre Dame I want to know if you like this joke yes or no that's all I want to know ok talk to you later bye

Parents // 5/24/13

Holly it's really I'm getting very anxious about your um um making a decision as to whether Dad is coming in June or not um I don't need to know immediately but tomorrow when I go to work I'm going to need to tell my boss so um today's Friday tomorrow's Saturday so um ok so it it's because I need to know what my schedule is I know you plan six months in advance and you're more important than I am but on the other hand um and you are you know I mean you're actively doing stuff and but but those times are open you know if you just don't feel comfortable about it don't worry about it just tell me but I'm just anxious about the whole thing um thank you love you daughter bye

James // 5/26/13

hey Holly it's James it's Sunday at around eleven thirty um I'm around all day today on cell I sort of understand what you're saying in your email from Friday not one hundred percent so I think we should talk about it overall we can work out a way to give you that transition that you're looking for without including all the parts but we should talk about what specifically you have in mind so give me a call when you get a chance and I'll reply to your email as well

Parents // 5/26/13

hi Holly how are you I love you take care bye sweetie all is good take care give me a call if you get a chance I know you're so busy you're too busy for your mom that's ok I love you I do want to know what Joey thinks about the joke about the um what's brown and lives in the bell tower though anyway talk to you later you can tell me if he thinks it sucks or if it has any possibilities bye now

Amanda // 5/27/13

hey Holly it's Jon um Amanda said you have a quick question about the P-Queue submission you can give me a call whenever you get this talk to you soon bye

Parents // 5/29/13

oh hi Holly it's Mom anyway give me a call when you get a chance love you sweetie bye

Steven // 6/1/13

Holly it's two thirty I would have called Joey but I don't have his current phone number for him he was supposed to be here at two o'clock and we're tied up waiting for him here and we've not heard a word from him so if you could ask him to phone and give us an update of where he is and when he's supposed to be coming it would be appreciated so I'm calling at two thirty right now thanks

[identifying information redacted] // 6/1/13

hey Holly it's Mike from Hyatt's you were just here I just want to leave you a message saying that the Rochester store is closed on Sunday however you can pick it up on Monday there and our Clarence store will be sending their stuff to our Buffalo store on Monday so um you can pick it our Clarence store is definitely open on Sunday I think they're only open until one o'clock but otherwise I'll have it sent in from Clarence and again the Rochester store is closed on Sunday but you can pick it up there on Monday ok and if there's any questions the number here is [identifying information redacted] extension [identifying information redacted] alright you have a good weekend alright bye bye

Divya // 6/2/13

hi Holly it's Div so I'm calling you um with a simple question about uh wedding times not about the music I was wondering if on the day of the wedding you would like to join some of the other ladies who are in the wedding party to get your hair done um I know you have your hair routines but if you would like uh a small treat the morning of uh it would be great if you would like to go to salon with us and hang out and get your hair done because why the hell not right um I was going to send you an email but I know you have a lot of emails and texts you're reading right now so call me back um or text me back with a response of yes or no or we can discuss it more in detail any way is cool with me but I just want to let you know we would love to have your company on the morning of uh just the girls so ok talk to you soon bye dear oh and Holls I should mention really quickly it would be totally a treat and my mom's treat specifically so she wanted me to call you and make sure that um you'd be in ok talk to you soon ciao

Parents // 6/5/13

hi Holly it's me love you just thinking about you I started doing a drawing each time I have lunch period at work I'm doing them of different staff at work anyway Dad and I had the most amazing salad that I fixed in the backyard it was a cobb salad and it just I had a just a little bit of smoked salmon on top it had all kinds of neat things in it it was so good it was you know underneath the lawn the swing you know this lawn swing the umbrella you know anyway so we had really nice weather here today it was beautiful and I miss you bye daughter

Parents // 6/9/13

hi Holly this is your mom I am looking at some roses they are absolutely gorgeous um and what their name their name is it's called Just Joey j-u-s-t first word last name is j-o-e-y and they are just gorgeous they're kind of a combination of pale kind of a pink a little bit peachy and then a darker a little darker pink inside and they're huge they're just huge and they're in full bloom and they're so gorgeous Just Joey you'll have to tell him talk to you later love you Mom

[identifying information redacted] // 6/11/13

hi I'm calling for Rachael [identifying information redacted] this is Donna with Olympic Rentals and I'm returning your call I'm gonna update that contact information right now and our email um if you send it to info@olyrents.com that's o-l-y-r-e-n-t-s then we'll get it it'll come to either any of us that's assigned to that that email and we'll be able to help you through there too either way is a great way to contact us if you need to call back thanks have a great day bye

(800) 322-4682 // 6/14/13

hi this is Chantelle [identifying information redacted] calling with Goodyear in the claims department eight hundred three two two four six eight two um it sounds like you spoke to somebody in our office yesterday and I do want to let you know that we do have a claim which is [identifying information redacted] um we're going to be sending a third party inspector out to look at the vehicle I just put in the request this morning so he may not be able to get out there until Monday as soon as I have a report back we will be back in touch with you thank you bye bye

Parents // 6/18/13

hi Holly hi Joey happy Father's Day to Joey's dad and I am so glad that you guys are there with Joey's parents Joey's dad of course and his mom and anyway um I would love to say hello to them over the phone but I know you think that's not appropriate we need to meet in person and anyway so in the meantime have a great Father's Day and we'll be thinking about you guys and um we are going out to dinner with Michael we're going to meet Michael at six and Dad gets to pick where we're going to eat it will probably be our neighborhood Mexican place which is very boring but I told him I would not complain so anyhow talk to you later love you and I got Dad um his favorite fruit tart flan or whatever you call the thing anyway um let's see what else um we've got a Father's Day card for him and um talk to you later love you you can call maybe around seven if you want seven our time that would be eight nine ten your time anyway if you get this message you can call us while we're eating talk to you later bye

Divya // 6/17/13

hey Holls it's Div I have a quick question for you about scheduling your hair appointment I have to decide between first thing in the morning or a little too close to the ceremony so I know you want to factor in your rehearsal time so call me back um the minute you have about two minutes to spare ok thank you

Parents // 6/17/13

hi Holly I work this is Mom I work for the next four days in other words Tuesday Wednesday Thursday and Friday and um I need to you know if if you don't think it will work out for you to have Dad come out in the first two weeks in July let me know because I told my boss I wanted to have those two weeks off starting the third I told her it would be ten days the third to whatever day that ends um but anyway um so let me know because she has to write out the schedule pretty soon um anyway so as soon as you know let me know ok I mean blah blah blah ok love you sweetie bye bye give me a call when you get a chance

(800) 322-4682 // 6/18/13

hi this is Chantelle [identifying information redacted] calling back from Goodyear I just want you to know that we did get our report back um and I do apologize we're not going to be able to help with the claim um the inspector found that the water pump bearing had failed from material separation I'm sorry material failure and that caused the water pump shaft to break the pulley had separated uh there will be a letter that'll get mailed out to you in regards to your claim but I do apologize again thank you

Nick M // 6/20/13

hey Holly I just got your message and I wanted to thank you for the invite I'm not sure whether or not we're gonna we're gonna stop by we're leaving somewhat early tomorrow uh to um uh sorry I just have man people on bicycles sometimes Jesus anyway uh we're headed back to New Jersey tomorrow uh somewhat early so um I'm not sure uh but you said I think from your message you said nine o'clock so that's not too late maybe we'll um maybe we'll stop by just for you know a beer or two or whatever but in any case again uh thanks for the invite and maybe we'll see you later tell Joey I said happy birthday see ya

Parents // 6/22/13

hi Holly guess what occurred to me uh well it sort of occurred to me before but it's totally I'm totally fine with it it's um it's that my seventieth birthday my big seventieth birthday will be on August third so Dad will get back on the fourth of August but that's ok I'm totally fine with it and um anyway I'm sure you guys will send me a beautiful message from back there and the fact that Dad's getting to do this is my birthday present anyway and Dad and I will he's never big on celebrating my birthday anyway so anyhow love you sweetie I'm I'm so excited that finally you know things feel better nothing's seemed set before it just wasn't right you know what I mean I hope to god the weather isn't too horribly excruciatingly hot anyway talk to you later bye sweetie

Mechanic   //   6/24/13

yeah Holly it's Dennis over at the shop I got your messages and stuff wasn't around during the weekend um we'll put the car outside so that you'll be able to pick it up or move it or do whatever you've got to do to it Holly give me a call back [identifying information redacted] thank you

Steven   //   6/24/13

Holly it's Steve calling it is Monday at about eight PM um I'm calling because I'm trying to get in touch with Joey about returning the key and uh his phone number that we have is now delisted or not working uh so if you do have his um his phone number or I sent him email on Friday and I haven't heard back from him so maybe you're out of town although I did see him on Saturday on Elmwood um so um yeah let me know if you have a phone number or else if you want to arrange a time with me to drop the key off with us again and have a drink hope all is well we have lots of news to report from Europe but I will leave it at that for now take care bye

Parents   //   6/29/13

hi Holly I was wondering how its going with ordering the Dad's tickets um I can go to the bank tomorrow before one o'clock and forward some money to your account but um you need to let me know how much other than that I won't be able to get to the bank it's gonna be harder let's see um I work Monday Tuesday Wednesday of next week and then I'm off for the rest of the week um but anyway the sooner we get this confirmed the better anyway one concern definitely is the heat you know Dad's had a heart attack and I'm a bit concerned what's not to stop him from going he he it's something he should do I mean um but um but anyway so give me a call it's really hot here oh my god and I have something funny I have to tell you something I did yesterday you won't believe it it's pretty funny so give me a call when you get a chance love you dear

Parents   //   6/29/13

Holly um call Mom I want to know if you've bought the tickets yet or what's happening ok talk to you later bye

Parents // 6/30/13

Holly guess where your father and I are at the emergency room at [identifying information redacted] Hospital um Dad has an infection we don't know what it is they just said an infection and um so right now they're doing a CAT scan of his belly we don't know if it's like an obstruction anyways his belly hurts in places and his kidneys ache anyway so he's been anyway give us a call if you get the message call the cell phone bye love you

Parents // 7/1/13

hi Holly it's Mom call the cell phone anyway

Parents // 7/1/13

Holly um Dad is ok he's um up at [identifying information redacted] the main [identifying information redacted] in room nine southwest room nine one one he has some kind of infection they don't know what the cause of it is but um they're treating him he was when he was we went into the emergency room last night at um well it was about seven o'clock and um he was getting dehydrated because he'd thrown up so much and um uh they ruled out it's not an obstruction his cardiac is ok which is good and um they it's in his gut and um so they're treating him they treated him with um intravenous of course and antibiotics so he's in really good hands and um I'm gonna work this morning but I'm coming home Michael's gonna be here about ten thirty eleven and um they don't have any um hospital beds he's not in intensive care he's in the next level down just for observation just to make sure he's safe 'cause they don't want to send him home with this infection um so uh they don't have that level of care at [identifying information redacted] Hospital so that's why they had to ambulance him up to [identifying information redacted] um but anyhow um yeah so let's see I have to go to work this morning so I'll talk to you later bye

Parents // 7/1/13

you know Holly you really need to listen to your messages more often this is really annoying I've been trying to get a hold of you your dad is fine he's in the hospital he went in with an infection his white blood count was way too high which meant his body is trying to fight an infection and we went in at seven a little after seven last night and I didn't get home from the emergency room until twelve

thirty at that time they ambulanced him up to [identifying informa-
tion redacted] Hospital because there's no emergency room I mean
not emergency room but critical care at um they don't have facili-
ties to care for him at [identifying information redacted] so um but
anyway he has an infection but it's getting better his white blood
cell count is um half of what it in other words the white blood cell
count was way too high and so right now it's half of what it was
yesterday when he went into emergency so that means he's getting
better so they've been giving him intravenous and antibiotics and he
is getting better but I don't know what the cause of it is um I sus-
pect his teeth because he has cracks in his teeth bacteria can get in
travel through his system but he doesn't think so whatever anyway
I worked today I worked four hours this morning and it really is god
damn frustrating that you don't answer your messages so anyway
um there's nothing you can do about anything anyway um anyway
it's just frustrating that you don't even answer your phone I know
you're so busy but this is ridiculous thank you bye

Divya // 7/3/13
hi Holly it's Div good morning um could you give me a call back
when you get a few minutes that would be really good thank you

Divya // 7/4/13
hey guys it's Div I was just calling to let you know um that we're just
gonna go in our backyard and drink some beers tonight with maybe
Nick and couple people so if you wanna come hang out give us a call
it would be great to see you bye

Parents // 7/6/13
hi Holly just Mom just want to tell you how much I love you and
I miss you and I'm just wondering how you're doing without a car
that worries me so much and I wish I had all the money in the world
and I could just give you one um let's see what else uh Dad is doing
better um his eyes you know are looking a little puffy but today he's
looking even better and right now I feel like I'm coming down with
a cold I'm laying in bed I got I um I have to get up you know like be-
tween two and in anyway the morning and when I get up um I end
up taking Billy outside three times I feed the dogs this morning um I
got a bunch of stuff I need to do today I have to go to the bank um

and I just want to tell you I love you I miss you and I wonder how things are going with you guys bye your mom

Eric // 7/9/13
hey Holly it's Eric calling hope all's well just wanted to touch base with you and Joe see what you decided for uh the lease feel free to give me a shout back [identifying information redacted] thanks

[identifying information redacted] // 7/9/13
hi Holly this is Heather [identifying information redacted] I was just calling for appointment you can just call me back my phone number is [identifying information redacted] thanks bye

Fred // 7/13/13
hi Holly Fred with your little Honda car I guess you might have got the word that we're still looking for a part water pump pulley only the pulley so I got the water pump itself changed and the pressure tested ok so as soon as we find that pulley we can finish it up Judy has done a lot of search so far we're not having any luck looking for a pulley so that's um forty bucks tied up in parts so far that's not bad and we're determined to locate the part eventually here it's Saturday the twelfth or thirteenth something like that alright talk to you later bye

Josh // 7/13/13
hey Holls it's Josh I was just calling um to talk to you real quick about the music I think Div already mentioned to you that we found somebody who uh could play the piece kind of a friend of a friend who's a music professor or something and just thought you know we could take that worry off your shoulders completely um I was calling to see if you could still bring um your keyboard and stand like we talked about the other night so when you have a moment if you would just give me a call back that would be awesome talk to you soon bye

Parents // 7/13/13
hey Holly do you have any idea I mean how much is this part is gonna cost because you know we'll need to pay this person before you can reimburse us so um give us give us a call and let us know because I need to have enough cash or whatever when we go up

there with money or whatever I can't do a money order banks are closed and stuff anyway ok give us a call Mom and Dad love you talk to Mom

Parents // 7/14/13

give us a call

Parents // 7/15/13

Michael got a job talk to you later bye

[identifying information redacted] // 7/19/13

hello this is the office of Doctor [identifying information redacted] calling to remind you of your upcoming appointment please bring your updated insurance card to your appointment please bring photo identification with you to your appointment the appointment is for Holly on Wednesday July twenty-fourth at one forty-five PM if you have any questions or are unable to honor this appointment please contact us at our office thanks and we look forward to seeing you

Parents // 7/19/13

yeah it's your dad Holly is that the right part give us a call and let us know

Parents // 7/20/13

hi Holly guess where I am at Grocery Outlet um I'm glad that the part arrived I'm glad that you're at the wedding and um I'll talk to you later love you sweetie bye and Michael got a job

Parents // 7/22/13

Holly please call

[identifying information redacted] // 7/24/13

hi this message is for Holly this is Tennille calling back from [identifying information redacted] we received your message regarding your previous medical records request from us but we just have a few questions that we need to ask you before um we work on that so you can just give us a call back at [identifying information redacted] extension [identifying information redacted] thank you

[identifying information redacted]   //   7/24/13
Holly hi this is Mary with [identifying information redacted] calling
on behalf of Doctor [identifying information redacted] I was look-
ing you were last seen here in August two thousand and six by our
nurse practitioner [identifying information redacted] at that time
and she is no longer here your records are in storage off-site we
can get them it will take about a week if you can have your doctor
um fax us a request for them but call me back [identifying informa-
tion redacted] extension [identifying information redacted] if um
you need any other information thank you

Amanda // 7/24/13
hey friend it's me just calling back sorry I didn't call you back earlier
this week it's been it's our last week of doing this full time teaching
job and it's just been like really busy and exhausting um but I hope
that everything is ok with you um as far as like your body and your
surgery that you mentioned um I'm just now leaving work but I was
kinda running around doing some stuff and I have to go grab Jon
but let me know what's going on with you I miss you too um and I
really hope that everything is ok and it's not a big deal um and that
you'll be back up soon um but if you get this at some point tonight
give me a call but if you're already off to surgery of course don't
worry about it we'll be in Buffalo after this weekend we'll be here
you know non-stop until who knows when so love you hope to talk
to you soon and see you soon and like I said hope everything's ok
sending you good wishes ok friend talk to you soon

Parents // 7/26/13
hi Holly this is your mom I'm dying to know how you are I didn't call
any sooner because I didn't want to bother you and I just love you
so much and I'm just wondering how you are if the surgery went ok
and I'm going crazy and um so I guess I'll call Joey I hate to bother
him but I just I just can't help being a mom anyway it's now about
six thirty here our time so six thirty seven thirty eight thirty nine
it'd be nine thirty where you're at and I just hope you're doing ok
I'm expecting you're at home I'll give Joey a call just not knowing is
driving me crazy anyway so um love you dear oh ok I'm gonna call
Joey bye I'm in pain not knowing how you're doing

Parents // 7/31/13

hi it's Mom wondering how things are going and I'm so excited about you going to Niagara Falls today with Dad and that you're recovering from your surgery and I'm just delighted anyway Billy's on my lap he's really getting thin oh poor little guy love you sweetie bye

[identifying information redacted] // 8/2/13

hello you have an important message from [identifying information redacted] MD at the [identifying information redacted] this call is for Holly Melgard we are calling you to remind you of your appointment on Tuesday August sixth at two PM if you are a new patient please arrive twenty minutes earlier to complete the registration process to cancel or reschedule this appointment please call [identifying information redacted] that number again is [identifying information redacted] we look forward to seeing you thank you

Fred // 8/3/13

hi Holly Fred a little after four on Saturday I just did a test ride fifteen miles on the freeway five miles around town and I think the old girl's gonna be alright no leaks you know it seems ok you can probably come and get it anytime call me at this number I gave you a good deal you're a family friend alright um don't worry about it right now if you want your car just come and get it give me a call we'll be here all night

(800) 864-8331 // 8/4/13

hello this is a check-in reminder from United Airlines we're calling to remind you that you can now check in online for your upcoming trip from Philadelphia International Airport on Monday August fifth just go to united.com and use your confirmation number and last name to retrieve your booking your confirmation number is i-k-l-e-m-p once again your confirmation number is i-k-l-e-m-p thanks for choosing United Airlines goodbye

(661) 748-0240 // 8/4/13

hey it's me my phone died you took the one good charger um but I'm calling you on Skype here's Skype so answer from Skype

Parents // 8/4/13

Holly please call this is Mom I'm not sure ok I was in traffic when you called and um I'm not sure I got the airlines right um I think you said eleven thirty but I want to make sure I want to make sure I get the airlines right um can you check it and call me please um it is not eight o'clock and you said I believe you said it was eleven thirty that Dad gets in but I'm not sure which airline and maybe it was eleven o'clock because I was in traffic it was hard to concentrate and um so please give Mom a call as soon as you get this love you sweetheart bye

Amanda // 8/8/13

hi friend it's me just calling to check in just wanted to see how your recovery and also your trip went and spending time with your dad and stuff um also I miss you and want to see you um I don't know if you're still teaching or not probably I would think we're working a lot and this job is kinda like driving us crazy um so I feel bad that we haven't been around and we haven't seen you in so long um but we only have one more week um so I was hoping maybe we could figure out a time when we could all get together um because I miss you and I would love to see you and catch up we're working today and tomorrow but we have a couple breaks mostly like lunch breaks but give me a call when you get this when you're free I'd love to figure out a time to get together and see you ok love you and talk to you soon hope you're doing well

Parents // 8/15/13

oh Holly yesterday and today just a few minutes ago anyway a man called and he wanted to talk to you and um the last time Dad said you don't live here you live in the east coast you like anyway but he didn't give your phone number which is maybe a good thing because you don't want some strange person with your phone number but the thing is that we should say to him well leave your name and phone number or something like that um that way we could give you his name and phone number and you could contact him if you want to or not if you don't want to but what went through my mind was maybe first Dad said maybe it's an insurance man and then I thought well you know maybe you have an insurance claim maybe he's trying to reach you because he has a question about your claim or something you know I don't know anyway but um give us a call that's all I know right now unless I try to find this number that anyway ok but I don't think I can do that talk to you later bye

Parents // 8/18/13
yeah Holly it's your dad did your care package come yet

Steven // 8/19/13
yes Holly it's Steve calling you on Monday eight minutes past noon I sent you some email and I am hoping first and foremost that you're well recovered from your operation uh the second thing is the urgency I'm feeling around the calendar we're now into the fourth week and you suggested in email earlier that you'd be fine by the third week so either way um if you can let me know how you are and where you are that would be very useful to me as I plan for the new term ok take care

Parents // 8/23/13
Holly call Mom and Dad and I'll tell you or call me and I'll tell you what I did anyway because Dad has less left over from his trip than he planned and he wanted to keep some for later and um so give us a call

[identifying information redacted] // 8/30/13
this message is for Holly this is Doctor [identifying information redacted] office calling just wanted to let you know um as of right now we have not received any records I'm looking at your chart if you want to give us a call back the number is [identifying information redacted] and to verify if they have the correct fax number it's [identifying information redacted] area code [identifying information redacted] if you have any other questions give us a call at [identifying information redacted] thank you

Katie's Sister // 9/4/13
hi Holly it's Nikki Kate's sister I was hoping to have a chance to talk to you briefly if you could give me a call back at your soonest convenience thanks

Amanda // 9/8/13

hey friend it's me um I just got your message I just wanted to call back and see how you're doing um I'm so sorry to hear the news um and I hope that you're ok of course don't worry about the launch at all you have more important things to worry about um but you know if you need to talk or anything definitely um I'm here we're here but I just wanted to of course yeah don't worry about next weekend and if you do wanna give me a call back if you have time um I'm around today Jon is taking this like fake GRE test right now so we have all the phones and everything on silent so if I don't answer that's why I just don't realize the phone's ringing um but definitely let me know if you need anything um and yeah I'm just sorry to hear the news um either way though I know if you don't want to talk that's fine too but I hope that we can catch up soon um whenever you get back I don't know when you get back but give me a call whenever you know is good for you and um I'll be thinking of you ok love you bye

Parents // 9/10/13

hi um Holly I talked to Katie's mom um I told her I said I just want to hold her I just wanted to you know anyway and um and cried a little you know she cried a little bit we cried a little bit anyway so anyway I said to her I said I know no words can I can say can you know really make a difference but I anyway we talked for awhile I told her that you would like to do an elegy for Katie and she said she would love to have you do that they'll have like you know the pastor or whatever do an elegy but there will be a sharing time and there will be a time where if somebody wants to go up and be at the pulpit and um you know share you know their own elegy or whatever they can do that and then there will be a time where they'll have like an open mic where they'll you know pass it around and share something they remember about Katie um and um so anyhow um I was talking to um um Rosie [identifying information redacted]'s mom I don't know if you remember her at all anyways she's a really really a sweet person um and she goes to that church our old church and I guess the Katie's family they're back there now pretty much they kind of go back and forth between that church and their new church but anyway so um so uh what else um I asked Katie's mom if there was anything I could bring she said if you make some cookies you know whatever that would be fine um but anyway I have a brownie mix I'm gonna make a Ghirardelli brownie mix so I'll bring those um anyway and put them in the kitchen of the church and um anyhow so I told her we'll all be there Holly and our family and I'm sure she she may have gotten she's probably gotten it from Nikki but it's better to hear it from my voice and I finally got the courage up to call her I was afraid to call her and um in talking with Rosie's mom it gave me courage to call her so I'm so glad I did um anyway um anyhow I'll talk to you later love you sweetie I hope you get this message if not give me a call either way whatever talk to you later bye

Parents // 9/17/13

Holly it's Mom Dad told me you called to say that you were home and that makes me so happy and um you must be exhausted and are probably sleeping now but I am I feel like I have jet lag and I feel like I'm getting my sore throat back but anyways I was at the bank um I got there about um oh maybe ten minutes to five I had an appointment with this woman um who's an expert in helping people refinance anyway so she helped me with it we're doing a refinance thing so we'll get a little bit better interest and um we'll be anyway the whole thing will work out better I'll say more about it later on but anyway so suffice to say I was there at the bank for what seemed like three hours easily two and a half hours I think anyway I didn't get out of the bank until um oh I don't know it was at least seven thirty anyway so um but um we worked on that she is really good but oh man I am so tired I'll talk to you later love you sweetie so glad you're home and um thinking about Joey and all that talk to you later bye bye

Parents // 9/21/13

oh it's just Mom I uh just talked to Katie's mom I haven't had a chance to drop off the plant or the note but I uh did call her and I'm going to do it today I called her and um and she said uh I told her later this afternoon and she said that's fine just call you know I told her I'd call before I get there and um I told her I didn't need to come into the house I just wanted to make sure she got these and I thought Katie would have just loved the plant and would have wanted her to have it and um but anyway she said that she wanted your address and I gave it to her and she wants to send you maybe a few things that were Katie's you know like sweaters or something and maybe a few pieces of jewelry um you know that kind of thing um anyway so um yeah she appreciated so much your speaking about your relationship with Katie and um so anyway I'll let you go talk to you later I'm exhausted I worked four days in a row and I only have today off I have to work the next two days which is not the easiest of things but Sunday will be fine because we're really busy but Monday just ugh Mondays are always a pain but anyway whatever um talk to you later um yeah bye love you sweetie bye

Parents // 9/25/13
oh Holly I just thought of something that's um it just sounds funny you daughter are the apple of my eye and Michael is the avocado of my soul talk to you later love you bye

(866) 219-2430 // 10/7/13
four three zero from the phone number where this message was left once again this is Rite Aid pharmacy services calling with a message for Ms. Holly Melgard please call eight six six two one nine two four three zero from the phone number where this message was left thank you for your time and thanks for choosing Rite Aid goodbye

Parents // 10/10/13
hi Holly it's Mom I'm at the University Bookstore I'll be here for another oh I don't know forty-five minutes hour at the most if there's anything you want from the bookstore let me know give me a call hope you get this message love you sweetie bye

Parents // 10/10/13
oh Holly when you get a chance give Mom a call it's your mom happy birthday's coming happy birthday's coming love you sweetie package is coming for one thing but anyway love you sweetie bye have some questions to ask you

Parents // 10/10/13
Holly happy thirtieth oh my god it's coming talk to you later bye

Rae // 10/13/13
Holly Melgard I'm just calling to wish you the happiest of all happy birthdays love you and I hope I get to see you soon bye

Brother // 10/14/13

hey it's me happy birthday give me a call back if you want bye

Parents // 10/14/13

hi Holly it's Mom happy birthday um give us a call Dad's got the phone with him and I'm in the living room he's just playing at the computer again so um give us a call love you sweetie bye happy birthday so proud of you our thirty-year-old young woman oh my gosh that must make me very old take care I love you but I'm happy where I'm at bye

(800) 947-5096 // 10/19/13

this is an important message from AT&T to discuss your wireless service please return our call at one eight hundred nine four seven five zero nine six you may also access your account online at att. com again our number is one eight hundred nine four seven five zero nine six or six one one from your wireless phone thank you for choosing AT&T

Parents // 10/31/13

happy Halloween um Billy is going as his own costume he is his costume is named skin and fur draped over bones beagle bones love you bye bye happy Halloween to Joey love you Joey I know I'm weird please forgive

Parents // 11/3/13

hi Holly it's your mom just missing hearing your voice um that's all I wanted to hear was your voice no matter what you say I wanted to hear your voice that's all I worked all day I worked three days in a row and as it's getting closer to the holiday season it's getting very busy and you know pretty intense at times and just missed just wanted to hear your voice to feel that you're my daughter and you're alive and that's all love you bye your mom

Parents // 11/10/13

hi sweetheart nothing urgent I'm at Swanson's working on bank stuff um Dad's out out and about and um Billy and Benny are in their kennels Billy is um getting stuck in corners all the time now he goes to a corner so he can stand up but he can't back up out so we're continuously rescuing him anyway poor Dad he's getting tired of this but um anyway it's a challenge so love you just wanted to let you know the condition of little Bill I don't know if he's going to make it till the time you guys get here um but I'm sure looking forward to you coming and um I'm making a little little things that will make things a little bit nicer when you come and um anyway getting things organized a little bit so I just keep plugging away at it love you sweetie talk to you later bye I'm using my cell phone

Parents // 11/15/13

Holly um last night we were eating dinner and Billy disappeared and he wasn't outside and we were looking all over the house anyway whatever you know where the closet is in the computer room I have a big portfolio cardboard portfolio there that's sticking out there and he got wedged between the the cardboard portfolio and the end of the bookcase the metal wire bookcase and um anyways so then I look at him and my god his rib cage wasn't raising I thought maybe this is it it didn't raise it looked like for a minute and a half and finally I could see a little movement anyways so Dad put him outside oh god oh another false alarm this dog is like a cat with nine lives I'll talk to you later bye love

Parents // 11/24/13

oh Holly when you get a chance give me a call

Parents // 11/27/13

Happy Thanksgivukkah to Holly and Joey this is Hannukkah and Thanksgiving are on the same day tomorrow and it's not going to happen for another couple of thousand years take care love you I have a poem to read to Joey if you'll let me Holly at some point

[identifying information redacted] // 12/10/13

yeah hey hi Holly it's Rick [identifying information redacted] from the financial aid office I know your appointment was for tomorrow but I wanted to get in touch with you earlier I was working a little late and I looked ahead to tomorrow uh I just packaged you yeah we got your FAFSA a while back I don't know why the system never picked you up so I'm glad you called when you did because we're getting towards the end of being able to put Fall aid up so you are packaged so you can go ahead and accept uh the loan that you want to use it so it is there um and um I'll call you again tomorrow at two thirty but if if you know if that's what you were calling about um your aid is up for you to accept now ok have a good night thanks Holly bye

[identifying information redacted]   //   12/11/13
yeah hey Holly uh it's Rick [identifying information redacted] again in the uh financial aid office I see you accepted your um your loan last night uh after I got your package last night so um I'm assuming you're all set with what to um ask some questions about so anyways I was just following up because we did have a time slot here but I'm assuming you're all set you have a good holiday bye

Macy   //   12/15/13
hey we're in Manhattan you should call us talk to you soon bye bye

Parents   //   12/21/13
hi Holly it's Mom I love you I'm going to be working on cleaning out your old room um anyway take care love you sweetie bye

Joey   //   12/22/13
hey babe it's me um I was just out with Lewis and Lisa when you called at the bar so but I am driving home now so give me a call when you get a chance um yeah glad to hear that you got in safely so yeah give me a call alright I love you babe bye

Rachel   //   12/26/13
hey Holly it's Rachel um my family was just wanting to know what your family's schedule was like and uh when you guys would like to meet up so um give me a call or text back ok bye

Parents   //   12/29/13
hi Holly uh just wanted to know if you if we should wait for you to eat or um if you wanted if you want for us to eat together talk to you later bye give a call when you get a chance love you

Ellie   //   1/1/14
hey Holly how was your New Year's just wanted to hear about it call me later bye

www.ingramcontent.com/pod-product-compliance
Lightning Source LLC
Chambersburg PA
CBHW062013040426
42447CB00010B/2013